44 HABITS TO HACK LIFE

PASTOR DIEGO MESA

44 HABITS TO HACK LIFE
ISBN: 978-1-7378702-7-2
Copyright© 2022 by Diego Mesa
www.ALFC.faith

Printed in the United States of America. All rights reserved. This book or portions thereof may not be reproduced in any form without the prior written permission of the copyright owner. The only exception is brief quotations.

Unless otherwise noted, Scripture is taken from the New King James Version® (NKJV). Copyright © 1982 by Thomas Nelson. Used by permission. All rights reserved.

Scripture quotations marked KJV are taken from the King James Version of the Bible.

Scripture quotations marked NLT are taken from the Holy Bible, New Living Translation, copyright © 1996, 2004, 2007, 2013, 2015 by Tyndale House Foundation. Used by permission of Tyndale House Publishers, Inc., Carol Stream, Illinois 60188. All rights reserved.

Scripture quotations marked AMP/AMPC are taken from the Amplified® Bible. Copyright © 1954, 1958, 1962, 1964, 1965, 1987 by The Lockman Foundation, La Habra, CA. Used by Permission. All rights reserved.

Scripture quotations marked TPT are from The Passion Translation®. Copyright © 2017, 2018, 2020 by Passion & Fire Ministries, Inc. Used by permission. All rights reserved. ThePassionTranslation.com.

CONTENTS

Introduction | 1
Work Hard, Rest Hard | 5
Just Ask | 11
Look For the Breadcrumbs, Not the Loaf of Bread | 17
Go Through the Door | 23
Ridiculous Responsiveness | 29
Creating Margins For Your Life | 35
Longer Than You Think | 41
Small Details Matter | 47
Challenge the Process | 53
Be a Curious George | 59
Don't Be a Sticky Person | 65
Why? | 71
How You Exit Is How You Enter | 77
Laugh or Cry | 83
Who Pulls Your Coattail? | 87
Unhappy or Hurting? | 93
Head Led or Spirit Led? | 99
The Great Departure | 105
You're Only As Strong As Your Prayer Altar | 111
Introverted and Distant From My Community | 117
Things I'd Do Differently | 123
Manipulation, Domination, Intimidation | 129
Too Confounding and Perplexing For Me | 135

CONTENTS

The Trio of Temptations | 141
Integrity and Image | 147
Grounded | 153
Adrenaline Laws | 159
More Means More | 165
Stifle Growth | 171
Clean = Unused, Dirty = Used | 177
Practical Wisdom | 183
Acceptable Noise Level | 189
Ambition - Good, Bad, or Is It All the Same? | 195
It Gets Hot Sometimes | 201
Structure | 207
All By Myself | 213
Sustainability | 219
The Three M's | 225
Transitions | 231
Without Faith | 237
Examine Yourself | 243
Scaling | 249
Resilient and Resourceful | 255
Engaging In the Hard Conversations | 261
Epilogue | 266

Innovate
Missio
Leadership
Cre
art
Solution
egy
Success
lysis
Visio

INTRODUCTION

We are all byproducts of our habits and practices, which influence our decisions. Sometimes, people go through difficult and unfortunate events that negatively impact their lives. Some people were born into unfortunate environments or had unfortunate associations, which resulted in unfortunate experiences. Despite all this, Jesus has given us the ability and opportunity to change misfortunes, regrets, disappointments, and shame into amazing turnarounds and outcomes.

Generations of leaders (today's and tomorrow's) haven't had many examples, models, and templates to follow and learn from. Failed leaders inside and outside the home, in the classroom, in politics, in entertainment, in athletics, and, I'm sorry to say, in the pulpit and church have not taught and lived at an ethical standard that can be admired and aspired.

In this book, you will discover truths, thoughts, principles, and ideas that serve as a guide to help you reach your destiny. They are timeless, ageless, enduring values for life, business, and ministry.

Why do many vacationers visit historical sites in Rome, Egypt,

Israel, and Greece? Perhaps it's because they love seeing things older than themselves—structures and art that have survived the test of time. Through this book, I ask that you allow me to take you on a journey to explore foundational pillars with a proven history of outlasting challenging times. The principles I share are not theory but conveyed from personal experience. I'm honest and transparent about what I did right and where I erred.

This book is dedicated to the decision-makers, influencers, and leaders of today and tomorrow, as well as hidden leaders who are unaware of their potential. If there's anything I've learned, it's never to underestimate or overestimate your value. My prayer is that Jesus will use this book to stir a person like you to reach higher, dig deeper, go farther, stand taller, and give more than you thought possible.

Thank you for taking the time to read this book.

WORK HARD, REST HARD

"Hard work beats talent when talent doesn't work hard."

–Tim Notke

Nothing can get done or succeed outside of hard work. Hard work requires busyness, activity, engagement, and doing something consistently. Hard work requires discipline to rise early and stay late sometimes. Hard work requires maximum effort, energy, and operating at your best. Hard work requires diligence not to give up because it gets tough. It requires you to get the job done, and no one should or is going to do that for you. Hard work is showing up where you're supposed to show up and being responsible for doing what you committed to doing, even if you don't like to or want to. Hard work will be judged by its effectiveness—making effective decisions, not just being active.

In reference to hard work, author Sam Ewing put it this way: "Hard work spotlights the character of people: some turn up their sleeves, some turn up their noses, and some don't turn up at all."

Hard work has no part in laziness, procrastination, neglect, or slothfulness. Whether your focus is marriage, parenting, exercise, good health, job/career, goals, dreams, forgiveness, patience, managing finances, or friendships, hard work is required.

It takes hard work to be responsible, to meet expectations, and to live a holy, virtuous life. It takes hard work to hold to promises, commitments, and deadlines. It takes hard work to keep your appointments and engagements and be punctual. It takes hard work to be caring, generous, kind, forgiving, available, and accessible. It takes hard work to live with excellence as a standard in life and give your best. It takes hard work to create something from nothing, to build something from scratch, and to have sustainability and longevity.

There are no shortcuts to hard work. There are no substitutions for hard work. There are no alternatives to hard work. As the Bible reflects, there is no harvest, go to market, and get paid moment for a farmer unless he works hard and smart at being effective. The Bible states in Proverbs 21:5 NLT, "Good planning and hard work lead to prosperity, but hasty shortcuts lead to poverty."

If you want to achieve something great, it will not come overnight or easily, and it will not be handed to you. It will take some level of pain, discomfort, irritation, inconvenience, sweat, or sorrow to be successful, but we all know that, right? That's nothing new, right? Today, however, we seem to have a shortage of people willing to work for anything great, worthwhile, or memorable in life. They want the results of hard work, not the pain it takes to accomplish their goals. They have a freebie or entitlement mentality. They think opportunities come quickly and easily. They believe success just happens or is given to them.

Jesus worked hard to fulfill His assignment in life, which was to teach, heal, love, lead, care, and be an example. His greatest assignment was the work of the cross—dying for mankind's sin. It was the work of suffering and sacrificing Himself so that mankind could obtain forgiveness. His was a good work done well. Jesus worked hard in His ministry from sunup until sundown, going and coming.

Benjamin Franklin said, "Early to bed, early to rise makes a man healthy, wealthy, and wise."

In addition to how hard Jesus worked, we learn that He also rested. May I add "hard rest," in literal terms. We see an example of the importance of rest in Mark 4:36-38. The passage tells us that Jesus left the multitude (people, work/job, email, phone) and got into a boat on the sea (a relaxing place), and went to sleep (took a nap) on a pillow. Wow! That's shut-eye and getting some zees.

If Jesus needed to rest, how about you? What is your boat or interest that you rest in? Where is your sea or the location where you rest? Where or what is your pillow--the place you can tune out and turn off all the noise, voices, and commotion around you? What do you do, and where do you go to experience undisturbed silence and tranquility? If you don't find your boat, sea, or pillow and make that just as much a priority as work, you won't be very effective or productive long.

Alan Cohen said, "There is virtue in work, and there is virtue in rest. Use both and overlook neither."

Resting is a must; therefore, you must mandate to do it daily, weekly, monthly, and yearly. It should not just be an idea you agree with; rest periods should be intentional.

Personally, I haven't had a hard time working hard. I score an A grade for hard work. I'm guilty as charged. My mind never rests.

It's always thinking, fixing, solving, and dreaming. However, over the years, rest has become a weak point. I score an F grade (maybe a D) for rest. That isn't balance, but rather like a lopsided teeter totter/seesaw. Unfortunately, I've pushed myself to the point of exhaustion and paid for it with my health. You've heard the expression, "Robbing Peter to pay Paul." Well, that was me. I robbed my body of the rest it deserved by not allowing it to replenish the depleted energy it desperately needed.

No one is the energizer bunny. Everyone needs breaks, timeouts, and rest stops. Everyone needs off-the-grid, closed-for-business, not-available moments, naps, and good nights of sleep—at least seven to nine hours. Everyone needs to recharge or refuel.

Effective leaders work hard but rest even harder.

REFLECTION QUESTIONS | Work Hard, Rest Hard

1. Which one, work or rest, do you do better?

2. Which one do you need to work on?

3. When and how will you start doing it?

4. What consequences or rewards relative to hard work or rest have you experienced in your life?

5. How would you rate yourself in the area of work and rest?

Action Item
If you are overworked, take a day off this week. Do nothing or do something you wouldn't normally do that is restful. If hard work is what you typically avoid, take this week to plan a new endeavor. Consider something unusual.

JUST ASK

"Asking questions is the first way to begin change."

–Thomas Berger

Our nature, driven by pride and ego, is to always look like we have our act together. It's called styling and profiling, image projection. It is seen in our homes, work, and church lives. But if we are honest, we'd probably say something like, "I don't know," "I need help," "I'm struggling," "I'm not what others think of me; I don't have my act together," or "I don't know what I'm doing."

Humility isn't always the most attractive characteristic to high achievers, positional leaders, and title-driven people. However, being vulnerable, honest, and transparent are virtues that God honors. God doesn't need us to fake it or pretend when we don't know how to do something. Asking questions, asking for help, and saying, "I don't know," is one of the most honest things a leader can do. Being cool, cute, and tough won't get the job done.

All of us have ceilings or lids when it comes to knowledge, wisdom, expertise, and experience. To ensure that we are not held back because of this, we must be willing to show ourselves vulnerable to someone by asking for help. We must stop pretending we know it all.

In the Bible, Peter was willing to be corrected by Jesus for his error, but that occurred because he asked a question. He wasn't concerned about how he looked or how his peers perceived him. He just wanted the answer to his question. *See John 21:21-22, Luke 12:41, Matthew 16:16-23, Matthew 14:28-31.*

When we started the church and began to rent, buy, and lease property, I knew I needed help. The church would not be able to grow past my ability or mentality. Growing to become a megachurch with thousands, I knew I had limited capacity and would need help and counsel to succeed. Even to this day, after all these years, I don't want to be an expert but a growing novice who asks questions of more experienced people. I don't care what I look like. I will raise my hands in a crowd to ask a question. I will call and meet with someone and ask questions. I will set up teams of experts to help and advise me on things I don't know.

I was an insecure teenager who struggled through school, acted cool, pretended to know everything, and didn't want help. But I'm not that guy anymore, and the hard work it took to overcome those issues drives me to be vulnerable, transparent, humble, and get the help, counsel, wisdom, and answers I need. Too much depends on me, and I can't allow ignorance or arrogance to rob me of my God-given potential. Realize that too much is relying on you as well.

Develop the art of asking great questions. You may want to begin with the following questions:

- "If you were to do things over again, what would you do differently?"

- "What are some keys that have made you successful?"

- "What traits were you born with, and what things did you have to learn?"

- "What was your greatest difficulty, and how did you overcome it?"

- "Is there any advice you would give me?"

A key to asking questions is knowing who you're asking. Consider their history, experience, achievements, and direct questions in those areas. Be sure to listen to the answers closely because what's said can lead to secondary questions. Remember: There's no such thing as asking a bad question. If you don't know, it's a good question to ask.

There's too much I would love to do, but I'm inexperienced. Some ideas and solutions may perish if I don't ask others to come alongside me. By not asking for the advice of skilled individuals, no matter the truth conveyed, there's a lot I may not realize. I must ask others to help me see what I'm missing and help me discover why I'm not succeeding.

Question: If we knew how close we were to the finish line or how easy it is to do or change something that we can't seem to achieve, that keeps averting itself from us, would we stay the course?

We don't want to fail in life and one day regret not asking the right questions or for the advice of others. Obtaining information can only benefit us. Questions help us make better decisions and experience better outcomes. By asking questions of the people who play a part in our lives, we can sift through the good, bad, and ugly answers and grow from there.

Don't be the person who continues to drive, all the while knowing you're lost. What would others call a person like that? I'll let you decide. If you're lost, ask for directions.

Albert Einstein said, "Learn from yesterday, live for today, and hope for tomorrow. The important thing is not to stop questioning."

REFLECTION QUESTIONS | Just Ask

1. Are you good at asking for help?

2. In what areas of your life have you noticed that you don't ask for help? Why?

3. What do you think will happen if you ask for help?

4. How will you benefit if you ask for help?

5. Who will you now approach for help?

Action Item
Each day this week, ask someone new a question about a topic unfamiliar to you.

LOOK FOR THE BREADCRUMBS, NOT THE LOAF OF BREAD

"God whispers to us in our pleasures, speaks in our conscience, but shouts in our pain: it is His megaphone to rouse a deaf world."

–C.S. Lewis

In my years of ministry and personal hardships, only a few times have I heard God's voice very distinctly speak to me about something. The first was when I was told to leave my former church and start ALFC. Another was when I was told to allow a private K-12 school to utilize our campus as their new home. Who doesn't want to hear God talk to them, especially during a difficult time or when a difficult decision must be made?

Many times, when we want to hear from God for encouragement, direction, or answers, we wait and look for the big, supernatural sign or something spectacular to lead us or confirm something for us. Many times, however, our situations look similar to Elijah's situation described in the Old Testament (1 Kings 19:11-13). Elijah was looking for the fire, wind, and earthquake to be God's voice speaking directions to him. However, direction came in the simple, still, small voice, not a bold, loud, glaring shout.

Does God speak to us with a spectacular, supernatural sign to confirm His direction? Yes, sometimes. But most of the time, it's not in the fire that one can clearly see, or the wind that one can distinctly hear, or the earthquake that one can unquestionably feel. It's God's breadcrumbs that are often revealed and show where God is, where God has been, and where God is taking or leading.

Breadcrumbs—the still small voice of God on the inside rather than on the outside—are powerful, profitable, and profound. However, to recognize them, it takes us not limiting God or saying that God is not leading or talking when He is through the breadcrumb moments. It requires being quiet and tuned in to God by being still enough to hear Him. It requires noticing the small stuff happening around us to see that God is with us, even if we have doubts.

Recognizing the breadcrumbs is not dwelling on the "why did this happen" or "why did that happen" moments but "what now, God," moments and the "I hear you; I see you, God" moments that appear in the breadcrumbs. The breadcrumbs become clearer as you spend time with God and develop a close, intimate, mature relationship with Him.

I'm not trying to be spooky, have you looking for messages in everything, or encourage you to stare at the clouds to see if they form an image that says something to you. At the same time, if anything outside of what's normal, anything peculiar, encourages you, uplifts you, or cheers you up, it might be God's breadcrumbs. These instances may help you to hear God and see God during difficult moments.

In 2008, when I was diagnosed with stage 4 kidney cancer, God taught me this truth during a very challenging time in my life. As you can imagine, being encouraged and comforted were huge at that time. I noticed random, unexpected things speaking to me.

One day, a hummingbird's nest was outside my front door in a bush. I did not notice it before that day, and I've not seen it since. God was telling me that He would take care of me like He takes care of the hummingbirds.

Another time, a group of fighter jets flew directly over my house as I walked out my front door. They were in V-formation. I'd not seen that before that day, and I've not seen it since. God was saying to me that He was watching over me.

Finally, another time I went into the market, and a woman at the register said to me, "You look good today." I probably didn't, but I took that as a sign God was speaking to me. I'd not had an encounter like that in the market before that day, and I have not had one since.

Stop looking for the big loaf of bread answers and see if the breadcrumbs of God are talking to you. Stop waiting on the big, booming voice of God and start listening to the small voice of God whispering pleasantries, love, and acceptance to you. The small voice might come in a passing thought, a lingering desire, or a knowing that you are to do something.

The more you learn how to become still or get quiet and become comfortable with solitude, just you and God, the better you will hear God's small voice, but you must learn how to shut out the noises, commotions, and other voices influencing you.

George Washington Carver said, "I love to think of nature as an unlimited broadcasting station, through which God speaks to us every hour, if we will only tune in."

Has God been speaking to you about something? Has He been giving you directions, but you're waiting for the big, booming, banging voice? Stop looking for the spectacular, supernatural, super-size, supercalifragilisticexpialidocious (in Mary Poppin's terms) direction, voice, and leading. Look for and listen to the still, small voice or breadcrumbs. It just might be God's sign or message of encouragement, inspiration, and comfort to you. He may be saying He is with you, He is for you, and He is bringing you peace.

Lastly, I want to be clear; this doesn't diminish the value of God's word, the Bible, which I believe is the primary way God speaks to His people.

REFLECTION QUESTIONS | Look For the Breadcrumbs, Not the Loaf of Bread

1. Can you see the breadcrumb signs of God's presence in your life?

2. What would the spectacular, supernatural leading of God look like to you? Have you ever experienced it?

3. Can you recognize where God may be speaking to you through His still, small voice in your life?

4. When was the last time you recognized His still, small voice?

5. What did you do after you realized it was God's voice?

Action Item
Write out an idea you felt came to your heart while reading this chapter. Additionally, write out the area(s) you wish to work on or grow in.

GO THROUGH THE DOOR

I've always said that where you start in ministry, business, or life may not be where you finish; just get started. Many people, however, don't take advantage of opportunities or invitations that come their way because that's not where or what they want. It's like they're holding out for the perfect job or want to start in the penthouse of success instead of starting in the basement of opportunity. Many want to hold out for the biggest and best position, title, or salary instead of gaining experience and allowing God to promote or advance them.

The Bible tells us in Zechariah 4:10 NLT, "Do not despise these small beginnings."

I wanted and dreamed of being a senior pastor, having my own church, and leading it with all the responsibilities. It would take nine years of working for someone in their church.

In that ministry, I was tasked with being a children's pastor, youth pastor, maintenance man for the property, and taxi driver for the senior pastor. I also cleaned toilets and ran errands, and I did it all on a small salary.

That ministry is where God wanted me to start. That was the front door that He was opening to me. Me saying "yes" to the open door of opportunity would determine if I would ever make it to the end door, the dream job, the desired end, what I wanted.

Walking through that door taught me valuable lessons on character, discipline, patience, and faith that I could not have learned with quick success. I'm so grateful that I didn't say no or hold out because I didn't like the opportunity that was presenting itself or being offered to me.

Don't have the attitude or think you're too good for God's starting position. You may have the degree, experience, or feel like a job is beneath you. You won't know, however, where God wants to eventually set you, position you, or place you if you don't take the initiative and say "yes."

Victor Hugo said, "Initiative is doing the right thing without being told."

Too many people stay waiting and never get to where they want to be or where God wants them because they're looking for the large, pretty, wrapped box instead of choosing and starting with the small, brown paper box. An example would be someone who wants to be in full-time ministry or positioned as a top executive, but there are no opportunities. The only thing available is a janitorial position in the organization. The individual can start in a lower-level role but have a long-term strategy in mind.

It's better to at least be on the roster or team than not, and an entry-level position is okay. Why hold out for door #2 when door #1 is good and guaranteed? You're not playing "Let's Make a Deal." The Bible says your gift creates room (space/opportunity) for you.

Through faithfulness, commitment, passion, and devotion as the best janitor, God and others will recognize an individual's attributes and notice how they can be utilized in an elevated role, but only after they've proven themselves in the lower-level role.

My advice is to say "yes" and get started somewhere. Have patience, display gratitude, and watch God lead you to where He wants you to be over time.

I've seen people in need of a job (money/income) to pay their bills and feed their family pass on employment opportunities that pay less than they were making in a prior role. I've seen them get deeper in debt as months of opportunity pass them by. They passed on opportunities that could have paid some of their bills, given them some kind of experience or at least peace of mind.

I believe insignificant positions prepare us for significant positions. Low-level roles qualify us for high-level roles. How we do menial jobs, with diligence and excellence, prepare us for dream jobs.

Never look down on an honorable role that God makes available to you. God may use it to qualify you for what's coming next.

REFLECTION QUESTIONS | Go Through the Door

1. Is starting small okay, or do you need big to get started?

2. Do you recognize missed opportunities of the past?

3. Although you were holding out, what door of opportunity is now available to you that you should take advantage of?

4. What stops you from accepting an opportunity/job that you feel is less than you?

5. Do you believe accepting ministry opportunities or having a job is better than not having one?

Action Item
Take action on what you wrote in the previous chapter.

RIDICULOUS RESPONSIVENESS

It's said that as is the pace of the leader, so is the pace of the organization. The organization you run or are a part of can't run faster than you. Your speed will determine the organization's speed or pace. I've always thought that way.

In the business of the church and the responsibilities I have, I've never wanted the ball left in my court. Another way of saying it: I never wanted people waiting for me to get back to them. I want to give them the answers they're waiting for or return the calls as quickly as possible.

Have you ever known someone who can't pull the trigger on a decision? Have you ever known someone who holds the ball too long without passing it? Have you ever known someone waiting for one more thing to happen, but when it occurs, they still need one more thing?

To be left holding the ball is when the leader has the organization on pause, held hostage, stopped because of procrastination, slowness, laziness, forgetfulness, or negligence. These are all tough words, but there's truth in them.

We should all be prayerful and thoughtful when making a decision. We should spend time with God, analyze situations, and seek good advice. Sometimes, however, it's not that we don't know what to do; it's the slow pace at which we run.

Geoffrey Chaucer said, "Time and tide wait for no man."

Steve Harvey said, "Time waits for no man, neither does a good woman."

I, like you, can get busy, and new challenges arise every day. I've learned that if I have ridiculous responsiveness to matters, I don't create unnecessary log jams. Ridiculous responsiveness keeps my life and organization moving forward. That's because people are not waiting for me to get back to them. That makes it possible for decisions and directives to be made, which keeps the organization moving forward. There's no unnecessary waiting, wondering, or wavering. All of that is eliminated by getting back to people as quickly as possible.

Our lives and organizations function by execution, which is getting things done, making things happen. This happens effectively when there's ridiculous responsiveness. However you choose to do it—reminders, personal assistant, timelines—is fine. What has helped me is my thinking and praying time in the morning. That's when I make time to reflect, hear, think, and plan out my day, and recognize who I have to get back to.

How would you judge someone's response time? How important is the response time of the police department, fire department, ambulance, 911 operator, or fast-food worker? Would you say critical, essential, or not that important?

RIDICULOUS RESPONSIVENESS

The Bible reveals to us in Luke 7 that John the Baptist is in jail, hours from being beheaded. By way of messenger, he asks Jesus a question (verse 19 NLT): "Are you the Messiah we've been expecting, or should we keep looking for someone else?" Jesus responds to John with ridiculous responsiveness (verse 22 NLT), "Go back to John and tell him what you have seen and heard...." Some replies are just that important. They require you to go to people who must make a decision.

Usually, when someone asks something of me, I get on it at that moment or the next break because I can have the best intentions and forget to reply. I'm always writing notes/reminders because I'd rather have the ball in someone else's court than my court. I don't want anyone waiting on me to get back to them, so I hit the ball back with my reply as swiftly as possible.

It's amazing what type of reputation you will earn when you respond to people with ridiculous responsiveness. It shows that you care. It shows excellence, and it shows you value people.

Keep the organization running smoothly and build a terrific reputation of respect for your clients, employees, friends, and loved ones by adopting ridiculous responsiveness.

REFLECTION QUESTIONS | Ridiculous Responsiveness

1. Does a quick response matter?

2. What pace do you operate at when getting back to people?

3. How long is the normal wait time to get a reply from you?

4. Does it bother you when people are waiting for you?

5. What do you think would be the benefit if you get back to people sooner?

Action Item
Take this week to be a ridiculous responder. If you already respond quickly, find someone who doesn't respond fast. Help them by being their example.

CREATING MARGINS FOR YOUR LIFE

Between words or sentences written on a page, there should be margins so that words are not tightly squeezed together. Margins also allow you to write new thoughts between existing sentences. They create space, and they make room for growth. They are areas of availability and provide capacity so that you may extend yourself.

Jesus had margins in His life. He could be interrupted from His planned, busy schedule/life. The woman with the issue of blood interrupted Him. At a wedding in Canaan, Jesus was interrupted by His mother. While on the cross, Jesus was interrupted by the repentant thief. He could have dismissed the interrupters, but He didn't.

Have you ever heard someone say, "I know you're busy" or "I don't mean to bother/interrupt you"? Do those statements imply that they believe you have no margin of time to help them? Maybe you are so busy that you have no time to be interrupted. Creating margins in your life means your schedule is not so overbooked that you can't take on anything new or help out during an unscheduled opportunity when a need arises.

Margins also allow us to catch our breaths between demands and the often fast pace of life to reflect, refocus, or reengage.

Don Herold said, "Interruptions are the spice of life."

Rich Wilkerson Jr. said, "What appears to be an interruption is often an intervention."

What are the reasons we don't allow margins? Is it because we believe we can make up missed opportunities somewhere else? Do we believe we can reschedule events by shifting some stuff around or shorten an undertaking? Do we believe we can easily prioritize a new thing over a prior commitment? Do we believe we can say yes to some things without condemning ourselves because we've been working so hard?

Many times in my life, I had the best intentions for being scheduled every second of the day. I was doing something and being responsible. I believed that was the only way to be productive. I prided myself on that discipline and was driven to keep it. When I didn't, I would condemn myself. But the truth was that because I was so busy, I didn't allow room for margins. Did I create margins to take an unscheduled phone call from someone who needed to talk to me or someone I would have loved to speak with? The answer is no; I was too busy.

My desire to be productive negatively impacted those close to me. If my wife or children wanted me to go to an unscheduled event or an activity they forgot to tell me about, I couldn't make it. If an invitation to an unscheduled luncheon arose, the answer would be no. I didn't create margins that said, "It's okay to go."

There's a song from the '70s titled "Cats in the Cradle" by Harry Chapin.

In it, he sings about a dad who never allowed time for interruptions created by his son. I eventually came to the realization that I, as the dad, was living the lyrics to that song, and I had to do better.

It's important to be available for people's invitations to celebrate life with them as well as accessible during their cries for help. It's okay to experience interruptions. It's okay to say yes to unexpected events. I've learned that God can use scheduled and unscheduled situations in productive ways which may benefit us and others relationally, emotionally, and in fun ways that we may not recognize beforehand.

Margin is creating time space, moving space, and emotional space to be available for new, unpredictable, and spontaneous opportunities. Margins help you avoid being so tightly restricted that you can't be bothered.

Consider an individual juggling balls or spinning saucers. When he or she creates margins or space, he can take on another ball to juggle; she can take on another saucer.

Creating margin is an attitude, a mindset that says, "I will live my life to allow space to be interrupted, to go off script, and that's okay."

Don't be so booked that you don't have time to take a phone call, pray for someone, play with the kids, go to the park, hug your spouse, spend some money, help someone solve a problem, go to lunch, take a walk, take a power nap, or simply breathe for a moment.

Ecclesiastes 3:1 says, "To everything there is a season, a time for every purpose under heaven."

Let's not miss God opportunities, God visitations where He needs us to be available to say yes. And when the time comes, and it will, let's have a welcoming attitude toward the interruptions, not a terrible attitude that reveals we really don't want to or don't like the interruption but only feel obligated to act. No! Let's celebrate the opportunities.

I remember when my kids were young and wanted more time, but because I was busy, I said, "Not now, I'm busy." No more of that for me, please.

REFLECTION QUESTIONS | Creating Margins For Your Life

1. Do you live a very scripted life with no room for margin or interruption?

2. On any given day, can you take on a God moment of interruptions?

3. How will you start creating margin?

4. What is your attitude about interruptions?

5. Can you begin to see an interruption and margin not as an inconvenience but as an opportunity? Explain the difference or provide an example of it in your life.

Action Item
Write out this week's agenda and look for margin moments. Do you have any free time? If yes, great; go out and create memorable moments. If you have no free time, figure out what you can trim.

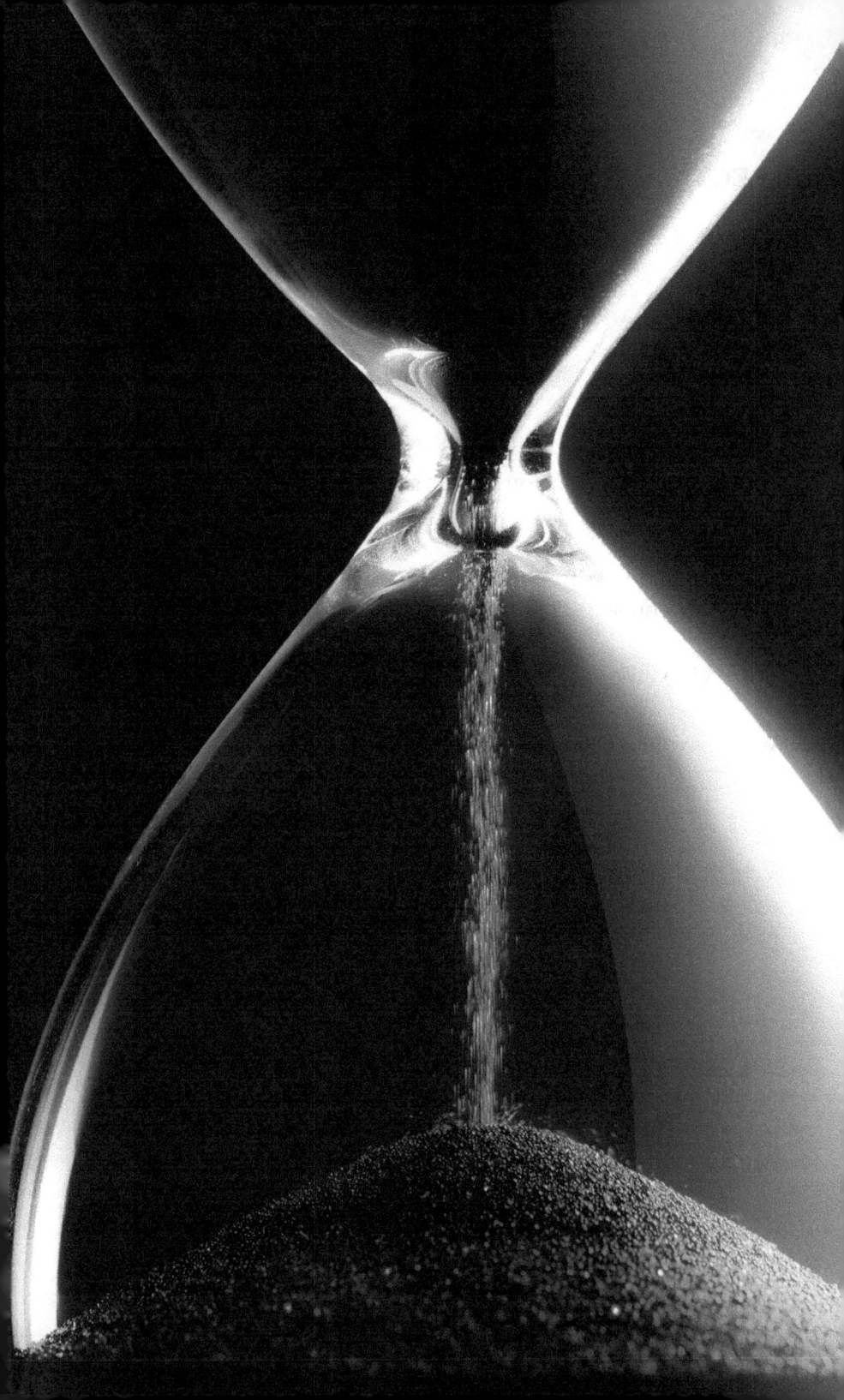

LONGER THAN YOU THINK

When we're young, we want everything instantly, right now, in haste. Patience isn't our greatest trait. We want "hurry-up" success, "hurry-up" growth, "hurry-up" purchases, "hurry-up" debt, and "hurry-up" promises. In our society, we're taught that the early bird gets the worm, and if you snooze, you lose. That may be true in some situations, but not all.

Here's a saying: "Do it right the first time and there doesn't have to be another time." That's true, and it speaks of being deliberate. It speaks of diligence and discipline.

Here's a thought I want you to consider. God is not as much in a hurry as we are, so we probably have longer than we think to do things right. Consider this when it comes to the first time acquiring something, developing something, creating something, fixing something, arriving somewhere, growing somewhere, and becoming someone.

We are often taught that we will lose out if we don't act fast. If we don't act within a specific time frame, then we are failures. This thinking can cause us to be impulsive, rash, and make mistakes. It can cause us to be emotional rather than practical.

Not everything in life is executed with microwave thinking. Sometimes, crockpot reasoning is the more acceptable approach. Things can happen or won't happen if we run too fast and are instant and quick about everything. Perhaps mistakes happen. Maybe no appreciation and gratitude can be forged; maybe no prayer and faith are developed. Perhaps no advice or counsel can be gained. Maybe comparisons to others begin to surface in an organization.

Here's the key: Take time, and it does take time, to develop a board comprised of the right people. Choose the right mentors. It takes time to study the successes and failures of others. Additionally, it takes time to get out of debt, develop a business plan, research and develop a project. It takes time to get good and experience great results. What I'm saying is to pray things through and process it all.

Remember the story of the plow horse and the thoroughbred? The plow horse is the one who is assigned the mundane tasks, and the thoroughbred is given the more glamorous role. Both, however, get fed at the same time. Just because you're first to arrive at the dinner table doesn't mean you get fed first or receive more food.

Consider the story about the tortoise and the hare. Taking longer to finish doesn't mean you don't cross the finish line or that you're not in the race. The winner and the one to finish last are invited to the awards dinner. I believe they are both winners because they are in different classifications or divisions, and so it is in God's kingdom.

Lastly, ensure you know how to wait well as you move toward your destination. Have a good, patient, content attitude, not an angry, fake, or miserable attitude. Whose clock are you trying to beat? Whose clock do you look at to determine the right time? Is it your clock, someone else's, or God's?

If you knew you would eventually get to where you're going, would you avoid situations or do anything different than you're doing now? Would you think cheating or shortcuts are the answer? Would you be as concerned as you are now if you knew for certain you would get to where you're going and experience unbelievable fulfillment and success?

REFLECTION QUESTIONS | Longer Than You Think

1. Do you believe you're in control of time, or is God?

2. Where in your life are you in a rush?

3. What do you think gets cut short when you're in a hurry?

4. Where do you want "hurry up" success?

5. Why and what is the cause or root of that desire?

Action Item
Write something you've wanted to do (e.g., take a trip, start a company, attend an engagement, buy a house), and provide an action plan to accomplish it.

negotiations,
indemnify and hold
of the liability or
This Agreement contain the
Agreement, All parties
persede all prior
agrees to indemnify
reason of the liability

SMALL DETAILS MATTER

In 1994, Abundant Living Family Church (ALFC) was established. I had been an assistant pastor at another church for nine years before starting ALFC. When I decided to leave that church, it was not well received by the pastor, which created a lot of hurt because of how I was treated.

When I launched ALFC, there were two instructions that I felt in my heart were given by God. First, I could not recruit anyone from that church to join my church. Second, despite the betrayal and how I felt, I could not retaliate in any form or fashion. Now, these two things may seem insignificant to the growth of my new ministry, and it may have been justifiable or excusable to do those things under the circumstances. I, however, had great conviction about how God instructed me to handle the matter.

In the Old Testament, there's a story about King David who worked to bring the Ark of the Covenant to Jerusalem but failed to do so the first time. He experienced much anguish, loss, and heartache. He succeeded the second time because he studied the protocol involving how to transport the Ark. Carrying the Ark involved placing poles inside rings on the Ark and placing the ends of the poles on the shoulders of priests who carried it. He did it the right way the second time. He obeyed protocols and was successful.

The rings and poles may seem insignificant to us, but they are very important to God. We must not ignore, dismiss, or disregard the small details regarding how we treat one another, how we do business, and how we achieve or acquire things.

Warren G. Bennis said, "Managers do things right. Leaders do the right thing."

There are details involving ethics, morality, values, obedience, and standards for how we do life and achieve in life that greatly matter to God. You may have seemingly won in life, but how you won matters to God.

I believe our church is blessed, growing, thriving, and existing not because of my brilliance, charisma, humor, and gifts and certainly not because of my looks. It's because of how we managed the details surrounding ministry/business in my season of hurt and offense. It involves simply obeying the conscience and conviction God gave us. It's what we should all be operating and leaning on, especially in the face of temptation (cheating, lying, stealing, or getting even).

Sometimes, God places mandates on us concerning what we can and can't do. We may be innocent in a situation, but how and when we handle it can make us stone-cold guilty of wrongdoing.

Because you believe you have a right to do something, does that make it right? Because you did it almost right doesn't matter. Song of Songs 2:15 reveals that it's "The little foxes that spoil the vines."

Plain and simple, if God doesn't like, you don't like. If God doesn't permit, you don't permit. If it's wrong, it's wrong. Pay attention to the little things you do or don't do because God sees, hears, and knows all.

A tough reality to accept could be that there's a lack of success, growth, and fruit in your life for a reason. Maybe there's much hardship and difficulty because you did something you shouldn't have that God noticed.

Matt Gutierrez said, "Pay attention to the little things. They're more important than you think."

Consider the termite. Termites cause more damage than floods, fires, and hurricanes combined. We often ignore termites, tiny bugs, but we can't ignore them because they eat away at our profits and productivity.

REFLECTION QUESTIONS | Small Details Matter

1. Is there any area in your life where you did things your way rather than God's way or ignored the details of a matter?

2. Do you think protocols matter?

3. Would God be happy or displeased by what you did or what He asked you to do?

4. Is there any area in your life you may have to go back and do it right?

5. Where have you allowed your emotions or pain to justify your actions?

Action Item
Add a timeline and specific steps to your "Longer Than You Think" action item.

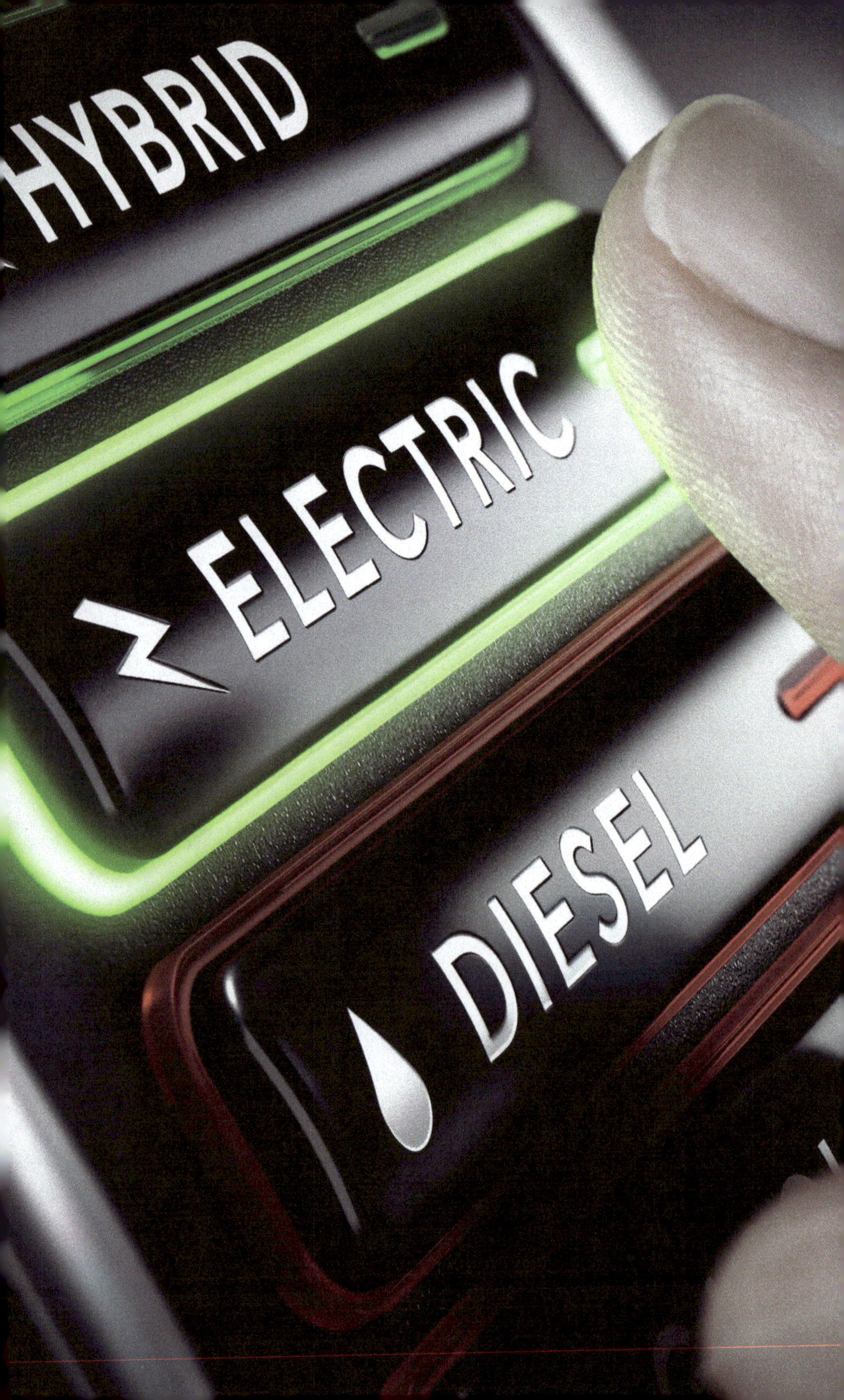
HYBRID
ELECTRIC
DIESEL

CHALLENGE THE PROCESS

Have you ever thought something to be true, but someone proved it wasn't? Have you believed someone was telling you the truth but later found they were not? Has someone ever given facts, explanations, or quotes that you believed and accepted but later found to be inaccurate?

We can avoid mistakes in judging matters or decision-making if we learn to challenge the process. In the church business world, with budgets, estimates, events/activities, disputes, and so on, we have learned to challenge the process to achieve greater outcomes. By challenging the process, we've altered decisions that could have cost more than we wanted to spend.

Challenging the process is not immediately accepting information given to you but carefully considering what's presented and questioning what's said. It's asking for something to be proven to you. It's asking someone where they obtained their information. It's not taking at face value what you heard. It's realizing and expressing that there may be another way of doing something.

Challenging the process has nothing to do with not trusting people, thinking someone is purposefully not telling the truth, or thinking someone isn't competent. It's not a personal attack against an individual, and it's not thinking you are better than another person.

Boyd Bailey said, "Lead problem-solving conversations to focus on improving processes, not penalizing personalities."

Challenging the process is nothing more than good stewardship. It's being thorough about how you process information or do business. It can be seen as another level of wisdom that puts you in a position to respond to matters appropriately.

Ecclesiastes 8:6 NIV reads, "For there is a proper time and procedure for every matter...." In the book of Acts, we see that the newly formed church challenged the process concerning why they should be circumcised, which was an Old Testament law. Ouch! Literally.

Challenging the process makes people around you better because it requires them to be very efficient and prepared for discussions. After all, they know you will be asking tough questions. Challenging the process is slowing down and listening to what's being said, then saying, "Validate that; prove to me that what you're saying is true," "Confirm that," or "Explain the details."

Challenging the process allows team members to ask questions, offer opinions, scrutinize, and use their gifts to help an organization without fear of retaliation. Everyone on a team should work to protect an organization, and challenging the process can expose things or people who are not accurate or thorough in their presentation of findings.

Keep in mind that challenging the process brings clarity, but it requires that you be able to handle the response.

We want to eliminate guesswork, presumptions, and one-sided opinions. We want to eliminate doubts, uncertainties, and "pretty sures." We want to eliminate insufficient research, facts, and evidence. Challenging the process respects individuals presenting information but encourages others to think from a critical perspective to rule out mistakes or speculations. Challenging the process simply fact-checks information that is expressed. It questions matters that sound good but are unfounded.

An example of challenging the process would be when someone says, "Everyone is saying this or that." You challenge them by saying, "Prove it." Someone else says, "This is the conclusion on this matter or the absolute." You say, "Please prove it." Another individual may say, "This is the only option for this situation." You respond with, "Prove it." By your response, you are asking the other party to investigate further and seek truths, including other possibilities.

REFLECTION QUESTIONS | Challenge the Process

1. In your own words, explain "Challenge the Process."

2. How can you do this in your organization?

3. Have you ever been guilty of giving or receiving unproven stats? If yes, what was the result?

4. What do you believe the outcome will be if you practice this principle?

5. How can you benefit by challenging the process?

Action Item
This week, ask someone in leadership a question to understand why something is the way it is. Additionally, suggest how it can be done differently. It doesn't have to be a perfect suggestion; just present a new idea. Afterward, write about the interaction.

BE A CURIOUS GEORGE

What I love about children is their curiosity—their desire to learn and try new things. Children are adventurous and audaciously daring risk-takers, and a great leader who can maintain a curious attitude, like a child, as he or she ages will always be necessary and in demand.

Everything around us is evolving, changing, and adapting. Sometimes the church, pastors, and leaders can get stuck in a particular style or method that is no longer relevant or effective. What they're doing may be very outdated.

According to a statistic, 70 to 93 percent of churches are not growing but are declining or plateauing. Why? What's the answer or difference maker? It may be refusing to try something new. I'm not talking about compromising values or morals, and I'm not talking about compromising the scriptures.

Companies like Tesla, tech companies, and those involved in virtual reality or the Metaverse stand out. Why? They stand out because of innovation, creativity, and new frontiers/discoveries.

Too often, we're not open to change or risk. A lack of courage exists when following through with innovative ideas because of what others say, think, or do. I don't want to be narrow-minded by thinking that my style, way, ideas, or methods are always right or relevant. I'm willing to try something new.

Will taking risks always result in home runs? The answer is probably not, but sometimes a single, double, or triple are good starting points. I heard it said this way: "I'd rather strike out trying than not get off the bench."

Connor McGregor said, "I'd rather shoot and miss than not shoot at all."

We could reach a younger generation by being open. We can reach a new customer or soul. Maybe we can reach a new culture or race. Perhaps we can do something better and more remarkable if we're willing to be open to change and adapt. Maybe we can be curious enough to say, "Let's try it!" "Let's see." What if it works? The knowledge we gain is better than not knowing. The risk is better than remaining stagnant.

I love hanging around my sons and younger staff members because they have different perspectives, outlooks, and interpretations. Sometimes, it's not easy listening to what they say. Still, I always want to be open-minded and welcome conversations. Sometimes, I can feel my narrow-minded, set-in-my-ways attitude arise, and I have to say, "Shut your mouth, Diego. Fix your face, listen and learn." I'm open even though it doesn't feel good, it's not my idea, or when I'm not used to something.

Jesus was a revolutionist with a new vision. He promoted women, hung around sinners, challenged interpretations of scripture, redefined the sabbath, and confronted religious leaders stuck in their ways of thinking.

Have an innovative and curious spirit about you. Constantly challenge the status quo concerning what you do. Never get too comfortable thinking you know it all, can't improve, or will always have growth, success, and wins. Don't let your history, experience, or track record of being right sabotage your future. Have innovative conversations or meetings where you invite people into settings to search out how the organization can change and improve. Foster an environment where everyone's ideas are celebrated.

REFLECTION QUESTIONS | Be a Curious George

1. What's the newest thing you've done?

2. Where do you invite creativity and innovation in your life?

3. Who are the people that challenge your creativity?

4. Why do you struggle with imagining?

5. What is outdated or declining in your world?

Action Item
Go out this week and do something interesting that you have never done.

DON'T BE A STICKY PERSON

It's amazing, when we think about it, how things we encounter throughout the day stick to us. Things like dust, dirt, lint, food, and insects sometimes stick to us. Sometimes these things are noticeable, and sometimes they go unnoticed.

No one likes unintended visible or nonvisible items on them. I wonder, though, how often we allow things like hurt, unforgiveness, or betrayal to stick to us. If these things were visible, like dirt, how many marks would you have? How dirty would you appear? How acceptable would those marks be to you? Would you be proud or ashamed of them? How long would you tolerate them on you?

Every one of us has been disappointed by someone, let down by someone, or taken advantage of by someone. Welcome to the sinful human race. The person that can scale past things like offense and not allow situations like that to stick to them long or change their attitude will be able to stay in the race longer with a good and pure heart.

Think about how many times Jesus was ridiculed, mocked, betrayed, lied about, rejected, hurt, and disappointed, yet He maintained His love walk.

Alexander Pope said, "To err is human; to forgive, divine."

Throughout my years as a pastor, I have had many opportunities to take offense toward staff members. Some have said things that weren't true about me. I've had church members say I did something that I didn't. I decided, though, early in ministry, that I would not be easily impressed or offended, and it has served me well.

Psalm 119:165 states, "Great peace have those who love Your law, And nothing causes them to stumble."

The key to keeping things from sticking to you is releasing things quickly. Be like Teflon, not Velcro, when things happen to you. Try not to internalize circumstances. Choose not to relive situations over and over in your mind but offer forgiveness quickly. When offended, immediately (like Johnny on the spot) ask Jesus to help you deal with it, and don't allow it to remain fresh by continuing to talk about it. Like Elsa said, "Let it go."

Secondly, rebound quickly. Don't stop what you are doing, don't get distracted, but put your game face on. Check and correct your attitude. Remind yourself of what and who you live for and think about that. It also helps to take a walk to clear your head and encourage yourself.

The next thing is to engage quickly. Pray for the person that hurt you, and keep investing in people. Don't insulate or become a recluse. Don't hide or say, "I won't ever again."

I've found that there's nothing worse than a bitter, unhealthy leader who has never gotten over their hurt. Hurt blurs vision; it keeps you from seeing clearly. You can try to hide it or deny it, but the impact of pain can show up in unsuspecting areas if not dealt with. It can look like a lack of trust within your relationships or an overly critical or judgemental attitude.

No one is perfect. We are all emotional creatures, which means we feel things. Situations impact us; however, we're not to allow things to stick to us but to shake them off. Just like we do with dust or dirt that gets on us, do as the song says, "Shake, rattle, and roll."

When mud is thrown at us (untruths, criticisms, judgments, etc.), we shouldn't try to wipe it off, or it will smear and become a bigger mess. Nor should we pick up a huge mud patty and throw it at an offender. Let what's thrown at you dry, and it will fall off. This may not seem easy, but it's necessary.

Tyler Perry said, "It's not an easy journey, to get to a place where you forgive people. But it is such a powerful place, because it frees you."

So, what's the truth to this lesson? Simply put, don't let the sticky stuff stop you. Shake it off and keep moving forward with joy, peace, kindness, and love. And remember, Jesus could have been offended by your offenses toward Him, but He forgave you.

REFLECTION QUESTIONS | Don't Be a Sticky Person

1. How long do you hold onto offenses; is it seconds or years?

2. What are you continuing to relive that happened years ago?

3. Are you more like Velcro or Teflon?

4. Who or what, right now, do you need to shake off because they or it has been sticking to you too long?

5. What would be the benefit if you let go of something or someone?

Action Item
This week, initiate a conversation with someone who has wronged or hurt you. Discuss the matter and clear the air.

WHY?

Kahlil Gibran said, "Ever has it been that love knows not its own depth until the hour of separation."

It has also been said that you will never know the strength of a commitment until a separation or testing takes place in a relationship.

Many things motivate people to strive, to work, to achieve, to acquire. There are many reasons why people stay doing and stay longer than others do in their commitments. There are many reasons people make sacrifices.

Throughout my years as a senior pastor, I've hired many people to work with me at the church and recruited volunteers to serve in some capacity in the church, allowing them to share their talents with others. Furthermore, a great number of people have attended services at ALFC or joined the church by making ALFC their home. As an employee or volunteer, some characteristics are admirable, like faithfulness, dedication, sacrifice, love, and generosity, which I'm grateful exists in all categories of people.

As it relates to employees and volunteers involved in ministry, I've often wondered why people accept a job or assignment at ALFC.

A series of questions flood my thoughts. What motivates people to be employed or serve in a church? What will keep them excited, grateful, and productive in ministry throughout their years of employment or service?

Additionally, I wonder, when people end their employment or service, what will be the reason? Will we see them again? Will they continue to attend and be members of the church?

Maybe my questions seem a bit erratic or paranoid but permit me to think through this openly with you.

In Philippians 2:22 and 1 Timothy 1:2, we learn of a relationship founded on loyalty. The Apostle Paul had many relationships with individuals who worked with him to do the work of the ministry. More importantly, he had Timothy, whom he considered a special son who showed and declared that he would not leave Paul's side.

Timothy wasn't just called to Jesus, Christians, the church, a title, position, or paycheck. He was called alongside a man named Paul. Hum! What did that relationship mean to Paul? Was that easy for Timothy to do? Did Timothy's commitment make Paul's job easier? Was Paul perfect in his leadership?

Over the years, when we hired employees, I knew they loved Jesus and were called to serve Him. I knew they liked the paycheck, benefits, bonuses, title, position, and authority that went with being an ALFC employee. They likely loved the status that comes with working at a church. Sadly, however, employees whose job performance or skill level no longer aligned with ours were gone soon after their employment status changed. They left the church. They left their brothers, sisters, and community. They left their pastor (me). I can't help but wonder why they were working at ALFC to begin with. What was keeping them here and committed? What was keeping them happy?

Suppose someone moved away from the area or was abruptly fired for serious issues. In that case, I understand why they separated from the ministry. But all things being equal, how do we explain others' lack of loyalty and integrity? How do we explain their conditional love? How do we explain their selfish decision? I believe all pastors must deal with this scenario, and I believe all employees and members must search their hearts for answers because it may happen.

Should a person be called to God, be called to a church, be called to a particular ministry, be called to a community of brothers and sisters, and also be called to a pastor that God gives them? If the answer is yes, what does it mean to be "called" to something or someone? I think titles, positions, and paychecks are cool and rewarding. Still, there's got to be something greater driving our commitment and dedication.

Let me land this plane. Why do most employees, when they no longer have a job or paycheck coming from the church, leave the church and don't return? Why don't ex-employees want to be your friend? I don't know the answer completely, but God does, so I will trust Him and be the best leader I can be. I will not allow circumstances to make me a less-than-healthy leader.

Someone once said, "When separations occur, they're not always amenable." Maybe I sound a little sentimental. The fact is we live in a world where we don't say appropriate goodbyes. People just walk out with no forwarding address. That is true of volunteers, members, and employees in a church, as well as family members and friends.

Paul and Peter had a dispute but remained friends. Paul and John Mark experienced a divide but remained friends. Huh?!

REFLECTION QUESTIONS | Why?

1. Do you allow what people do to you to get in between you and your relationship with God?

2. Have you ever stopped on God because of how someone failed you?

3. The next time man fails you, what will you do?

4. How will you seek healing if man fails you?

5. What do you believe will result if you stop on God?

Action Item
Choose a day to spend one hour with God this week in a place different from the typical space. Use part of that time to write down situations you should have handled differently, then forgive yourself.

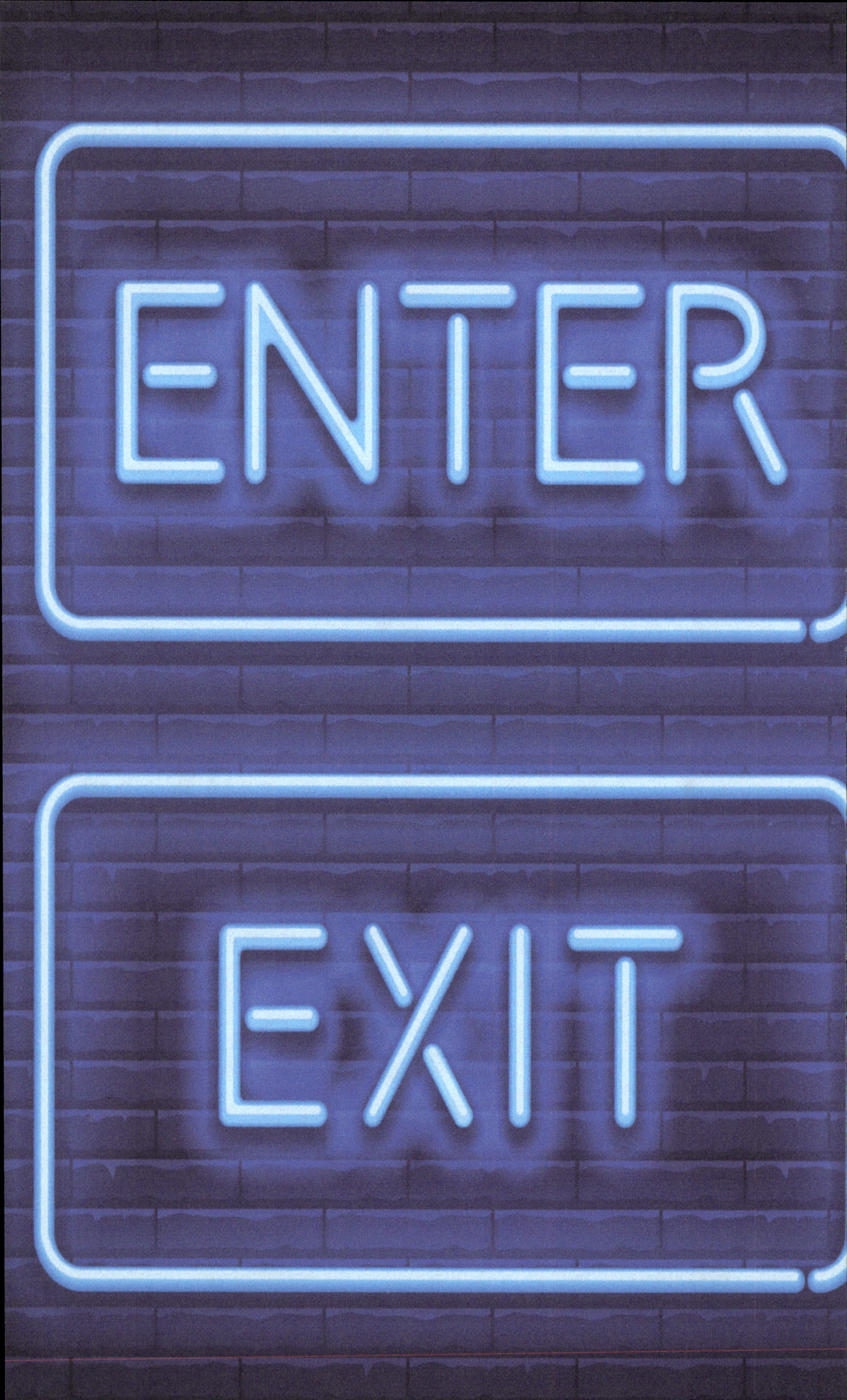
ENTER
EXIT

HOW YOU EXIT IS HOW YOU ENTER

1 Corinthians 14:40 NLT states, "But be sure that everything is done properly and in order."

Oftentimes, we are clearly aware of how we entered something, but we pay little attention to how we exited something. We are so excited about the entrance or the new that we pay little attention or place little importance on how we exited or left something. That could be a job, church, family, or relationship.

We often think it's more important or a priority for us to think about entering a new door or opportunity than to be concerned about how we left or exited an old one. However, if we haven't exited right, how can we enter right?

So often, we think moving on to something new, exciting, or fun is the right move. Although new experiences may bring out positive emotions within us, or maybe it's God's will, how we exit, leave, depart, move on, retire, evacuate, exodus, say farewell or goodbye means everything. It is huge in God's sight and can't be ignored.

One time, I was voluntarily fired from a job, and I left the job with a ton of bitterness and resentment. Some time passed, and I felt challenged by God to meet up with my former boss because I heard the person was sick and moving out of the state. I accepted the challenge. We met and talked for two hours. We reminisced about the fifteen years I was employed by this individual. We laughed and cried, and I thanked them for hiring a twenty-two-year-old kid and let them know that I appreciated their investment in me. Although I never received an apology or the admission of wrong that I was expecting, I exited right, with a guilt-free conscience, and ran into my next job and season in life.

Sometimes, people exit a marriage, job, friendship, church, promise, or commitment with bitterness, resentment, unforgiveness, anger, hostility, hatred, or the slam of a door. They don't do good or exit well. They don't return and apologize for how they exited, which may have included gossiping, division, strife, complaining, or destruction. They are only focused on the new season, new marriage, new church, new job, and new friends (I believe you're getting the picture).

If we don't exit correctly, we bring our emotional baggage, unresolved issues, personality/character flaws, and lack of closure into new endeavors.

Here is what I know: You can't hide an unresolved issue or pretend it doesn't exist or matter. Emotions will flare up and probably in the worse way. God can't promote, use, bless, prosper, or favor you for your next season if you don't leave right and respectfully.

Sometimes, we exit a place because of awful situations, but that doesn't excuse bad behavior or destructive attitudes. Poor conduct can cause us to tear down or rip apart accumulated advancements. Sometimes, righteous exits may not be received well. Still, at least you can leave with honor, knowing you acted Christ-like, even though the other party behaved contrarily.

I believe Jesus is a God of protocols, and if we don't follow righteous protocols, God can't bless our future progress. Exiting right is about integrity, ethics, honor, and respect, and sometimes has nothing to do with the other party but everything to do with you and God. God sees everything, hears everything, knows everything, and records everything. Humbling your pride and exiting appropriately can ensure blessings. You can run into your next season with great expectations and anticipation.

Don't leave a mess or trash when you exit somewhere. Leave with no confusion or waste behind.

Robert Fulghum said, "Clean up your own mess."

It has also been said, "Your habits are a reflection of you. Clean up and pick up after yourself."

If you didn't exit a situation right, maybe repentance toward God and an apology to those you left is necessary. Having good closure is the goal, not leaving with unresolved issues, which leaves the door open for future convictions of the heart.

REFLECTION QUESTIONS | How You Exit Is How You Enter

1. When things get tough, do you think about exiting rather than staying?

2. Do you believe that how you exit matters?

3. What would a good exit look like to you versus a bad exit?

4. Are you good or bad at exiting?

5. Is there any exit you need to revisit and do right?

Action Item
Share with someone close in your community something that's hurting you.

LAUGH OR CRY

Marjorie Pay Hinckley said, "The only way to get through life is to laugh your way through it. You either have to laugh or cry. I prefer to laugh. Crying gives me a headache."

Life is tough; there's no mystery there. That's not a new revelation. Life is filled with joy and happiness, including love, marriage, family, success, and favorable outcomes. Life is also filled with sadness, loss, failure, defeat, and pain. I believe both emotional situations (joy and sorrow) are understandable, and the joy-to-sorrow moments are seasons. But I want to give you another leadership perspective regarding these emotions.

When things go wrong, not as predicted or expected, instead of crying about it, let's laugh. Don't stop reading this. Let me explain further.

Tough times are inevitable. Some are predictable, and others are unpredictable, but instead of the negative emotions taking you somewhere you may regret or to an unhealthy place, laugh about it. It's not a laugh of denial implying that things aren't real, challenging, or discouraging.

Here's the statement that I say to myself: "If you don't just laugh about it, you will cry."

Proverbs 17:22 AMP says, "A happy heart is good medicine, and a joyful mind causes healing...."

So many times, people have made promises to me to help or to show up for something, to stay with me, to serve with me, but they didn't come through. Instead of crying in pain, I laugh because people are human, with all their frailties and flaws.

When someone I love turns their back on me or fabricates lies, I can cry or laugh. My laughter is saying, "God, help them; God, forgive them; God, show them; God, teach them; God, help me, and God, teach me."

When church employees are released for downsizing, underperforming, or disciplinary action but decide they don't like you anymore, don't call you "Pastor" anymore, leave and don't come to church anymore, choose to laugh, or you may cry in pain. Laughing can act as a buffer against unhealthy and inappropriate emotions.

A response in laughter can be seen outwardly, but it's mainly about impacting your thinking. See laughter as a positive response to the things that could get under your skin. Laughing may be the thing that keeps you from flying off the handle or becoming bitter, ugly, or hateful. You may want to say this phrase amid adversity as a healing/recovery statement: "Laugh, or you'll cry." Say it now for practice.

People are people, and they do people stuff. Sometimes, they are massive losses. Sometimes, they're bad investments or decisions. Sometimes, they are big lawsuits. Sometimes, they are bad social media comments. Sometimes, they are family but don't act like family. Sometimes, they are friends who aren't friends. Sometimes, they are mean, ugly, weird, or less-than-great people who will fail you. Learn to laugh at it, laugh through it, and laugh about it.

Take laugh breaks. Turn the tide or atmosphere of a horrendous situation to something positive. Laugh or cry; it's your choice.

REFLECTION QUESTIONS | Laugh or Cry

1. When is a good time to laugh? Is it only when you experience fun situations or also in bad times?

2. Do you believe laughing can help you deal with negative emotions? How so?

3. Do you think laughing at issues will stop or limit your complaining?

4. Can you see laughing as a medicine for your feelings?

5. Are you more of a laugher or crier?

Action Item
Write the names of people you can cry in front of—those you can share your hurts and pains with. Furthermore, write why you can express your emotions with them.

WHO PULLS YOUR COATTAIL?

I believe God the Father is accountable to the Godhead (Trinity). I believe Jesus is accountable to the Godhead. I believe the Holy Spirit is accountable to the Godhead (John 5:19, John 8:29). Accountability is huge in the kingdom of God and should be a must in our lives.

Too many people are what I call "freelancers" or "free agents." They appear to serve or work for the coach (Jesus). They are a part of the team but do their own thing and play by different rules. They're not as coachable as everyone else. They don't check in like everyone else, and they don't receive instructions like everyone else. They don't want to be evaluated or questioned like everyone else. They don't like to be chastened or confronted like everyone else. There may be ignorance or arrogance about them. I don't know.

Stephen Covey said, "Accountability breeds responsibility."

Thomas Paine said, "A body of men holding themselves accountable to nobody ought not to be trusted by anybody."

Many great leaders have fallen, or will fall, because of a lack of accountability to marriage, family, friends, mentors, pastors, boards, and other authority figures. Sometimes, people start off teachable, responsible, humble, and accountable, but when they reach a certain age, success, status, or achievement, they think they have arrived. They don't need to be accountable anymore. They don't ask permission, give an account of their actions, or come under scrutiny. They don't listen to correction, advice, or counsel anymore. Let's not repeat the mistakes of others.

Once, a guy visited our church and gave me a word of correction. I asked him about the location of the church he was attending and the name of his pastor. He didn't like me questioning him. However, to be in authority, you must be under authority.

Accountability is God's plan to protect our lives, and it protects us from temptation, haughtiness, arrogance, pride, selfishness, and deception. I don't know about you, but I believe we perform better when someone is watching or checking in with us.

I always want to be in a position where people assigned to me by God as accountability partners can pull my coattail when I'm headed in the wrong direction. Everyone has blind spots, weaknesses, and temptations. That's why God gives us others who see what we don't see. They may notice what we don't notice.

Accountability allows authority figures or close friends to question our motives, actions, and habits. Accountability is letting someone hold us responsible for our weaknesses, vulnerabilities, and temptations. Accountability is letting someone get in our business.

Question: When you are faced with a major decision, to whom do you go to bounce the decision off when you want a second opinion? Who is your sign-off person?

Think of people you know who have fallen and lost their influence or position. Why did that happen? Could it have been avoided? What could they have done differently?

One of the Beatitudes in the Bible speaks of meekness. That means teachable, and that does not merely imply learning new stuff. It's being extremely correctable when confronted. Being correctable means you're close enough to someone who can confront you when you're wrong.

We need strong people who aren't impressed or intimidated by who we are and will keep us in check. They will speak the truth to us when we need it. The Bible encourages us to confess our sins to one another (James 5:16). What if we confess our temptations toward sin as well?

REFLECTION QUESTIONS | Who Pulls Your Coattail?

1. Who can you ask to be your accountability partner?

2. Have you had conversations with your accountability partner, yet you continue to doubt their role in your life?

3. When was the last time someone corrected you, and how did you handle that?

4. What stops people from being accountable to anyone?

5. Do you have people you watch out for and correct or pull their coattails?

Action Item
Take your accountability partner to lunch and discuss what you've gained so far by reading this book.

UNHAPPY OR HURTING?

Jesus said, "The poor you have with you always." What if poor means more than financially deficient? Poor could include someone with a poor attitude who may not want to get better but likes being that way.

Have you ever considered that there's a difference between an unhappy person and a hurting person? We will encounter different types of people in life, and distinguishing between them can make all the difference. We will all encounter troubled people and occasionally be troubled people. On our jobs as well as in churches, families, and friendships are where we find them.

Question: Are we called to help everyone? Should we help everyone? Can we help everyone? How much help should we offer to someone? How long should our commitments be to someone? Are any conditions or expectations placed on those we're trying to help?

I recognize that, from a distance, dirt and mold can look the same on a wall, but there's a vast difference between the two. One can easily be wiped away or cleaned; the other is very serious and deeply embedded. Let's see if we can navigate the differences between unhappy and hurting so we can have healthy perspectives, outcomes, and relationships with people.

Unhappy people and hurting people may look the same when they come into our lives. They've been wounded by something, complaining about something, angry at something, or discouraged and desponded over something. They may appear lost and without hope or direction. They may be willing to quit, give up, and never commit to something again. They may feel betrayed, abandoned, misused, taken advantage of, and unappreciated.

Here's the "drop the mic" big difference: As you question, counsel, and coach them, and spend a lot of time with them, one will get better (healed) and move on from the negative, destructive, unhealthy events, and the other will stay the same. The other will continue to talk about what took place, live in it, and act it out. They continue to reengage and revisit what occurred, no matter how much you encourage them to move on and give them the tools to do so.

You see, hurting people want to get better and will do whatever it takes to get better. They will show signs of improvement. They will show appreciation and value your time and efforts. They will let Jesus heal them of their wounds, and sincerely hold themselves accountable as you do. They will become strong and productive in God's kingdom. The hurting will work to get whole, but the unhappy is another story.

The unhappy come to you unhappy, and when they must leave you, they will leave unhappy. They remain the same with the same issues, negative emotions, and complaints. They will not confront the issues they face and will not hold themselves responsible for their attitudes. They show little to no signs of improvement. And here's the tragedy: They will drain the life out of you. If you let them, they will consume much of your energy, emotions, and time.

I try to keep everyone happy, and the problem is when I do that, I become unhappy.

If someone constantly makes you unhappy, you must develop the courage to let that person go. Understand you aren't anyone's savior or martyr. You can't help people if they don't want to be helped. We can still love them, pray for them, and check in occasionally. Still, you must set boundaries, or you will be taken advantage of, and it will frustrate and drain you.

We are all called to the hurting, not the unhappy. I will try to help both, but the moment I notice someone doesn't want to get better, I must use wisdom and have the courage to release them by having a hard conversation about the future and what our relationship will look like. I may suggest a professional therapist for the issue they are facing.

Recognizing that you may not be the one God will use to help an individual can be liberating. Realize that God can use someone other than you. You're not abandoning the individual, which should bring you peace of mind.

REFLECTION QUESTIONS | Unhappy or Hurting?

1. Describe, in your own words, the difference between the unhappy and the hurting.

2. Do you think it's okay to show different commitments to the two?

3. Have you ever helped an unhappy or hurting person?

4. What advice can you give a hurting person, a solution that may not involve you?

5. Do you have encounters you can share about this topic? What instances of unhappy versus hurting have you experienced?

Action Item
Do something fun this week and invite someone to join you.

HEAD LED OR SPIRIT LED?

I appreciate education, books, and intellectuals. I respect logic and rationale expressed through a gifted mind. I value natural memory and remembrance of things learned. I appreciate excellent comprehension and great understanding to grasp what's taught. People who possess these skills are to be admired for their high IQ, grade point averages, earned degrees, statuses, and achievements. We should all perhaps strive for these.

I believe there is head knowledge that should be acquired, but I believe spiritual discernment should also be attained.

Oftentimes, great emphasis is placed on the head or mind of a man, but we neglect the spirit of a man. It's the part of a person that can be influenced, developed, and affected by the Holy Spirit's leading and direction. That may look like unction, urges, compulsion, and empowerment.

Romans 8:14, John 14:26, and Acts 8:29 are a few scriptures that talk about how the Holy Spirit participates in a believer's life and is completely available and accessible.

I will admit that learning from a book or concepts in a classroom was hard for me. I struggled for years with the traditional way of learning and comprehending. However, depending on the Holy Spirit to help me navigate through tough decisions has served me well.

Learning naturally through logic/reasoning and trying to figure out everything has its limits and reservations (Proverbs 3:7). Listening to the Holy Spirit's guidance is an art, a gift of discipline that is much needed and unlimited.

Hudson Taylor said, "We give too much attention to method and machinery and resources, and too little to the source of power [the Holy Spirit]."

The Holy Spirit's leading has helped me greatly. His guidance has helped me to do things that required excellent timing in making decisions, strategy, and having hard conversations. I've relied on Him to show me what to do, how to act, and when to speak out on hot issues. He has shown me how to respond to conflict, including hurtful people who have expressed hateful words. I've relied on Him for vision, the flow of a worship service, ideas, as well as property acquisitions.

There is power in the Holy Spirit's leading. The world feeds our natural mind, but the Holy Spirit feeds and fuels our spirit.

When you receive a download from the Holy Spirit, you know things that didn't come from a classroom, book, or seminar. That knowledge comes through inspiration from the Holy Spirit. This strong knowing or premonition can come when you're thinking about what to do or in random, unexpected moments. It can come as a still, small voice from inside you, permeating your mind with the clarity of ideas. Know that the developed practice or discipline comes through an active prayer life and asking the Holy Spirit to guide your decisions.

This valuable relationship I'm describing might be challenging for a non-Christian and those who don't know the Bible to understand. It may even sound farfetched, but it is an amazing gift that can help us to react appropriately, without logic, to situations we face.

Oftentimes, when someone has a strong, intellectual mind, it's hard to depend on the leading and unction of the Holy Spirit. It's as if their strength produces their weakness. They've developed one part of themselves (mind), which caused an underdeveloped spirit.

A.W. Tozer said, "If the Holy Spirit was withdrawn from the church today, 95 percent of what we do would go on and no one would know the difference. If the Holy Spirit had been withdrawn from the New Testament church, 95 percent of what they did would stop and everyone would know the difference."

How often does something look good from a distance but up close, or in hindsight, it wasn't good for you? What if you could pray about something and ask the Holy Spirit to reveal the truth or an answer prior to your decision? What if you choose to wait on God for direction or answers? Maybe you can see it as more of a sixth sense or similar to a blind person's dependence on the gentle nudge of his K9 companion that provides direction.

Should we be more dependent and dominated by our natural minds to decide something based on logic or experience? Is it possible to be just as gifted by allowing our spirit to guide us with the help of the Holy Spirit's leading, voice, witness, and direction?

When the Spirit leads you, it may come on as a strong knowing of what to do, how to do it, when to do it, why to do it, and where to do it. It's a knowing that didn't come from the influence of a person. The Holy Spirit is leading you, guiding you, and showing you.

REFLECTION QUESTIONS | Head Led or Spirit Led?

1. Do you think the Holy Spirit can guide you into a decision?

2. Do you think you depend more on your mind or spirit?

3. What can you do to get better at depending on the Holy Spirit?

4. Do you have examples of the Holy Spirit's leading in your life?

5. How can depending on the guidance of the Holy Spirit help you?

<u>Action Item</u>
One day this week, sit in silence for ten minutes. Write down the thoughts that aren't typical. Afterward, note connections between usual thoughts and what you described as unusual.

THE GREAT DEPARTURE

John 6:66 reads, "From that time many of His disciples went back and walked with Him no more."

Chris Gore said, "When life throws you a curve ball, you will end up saying, 'God, what are you doing to me.' We end up blaming God as opposed to allowing the goodwill of God to navigate us through the situation."

Here's a truth: Man fails us, but God never fails us. If that's true, and it is, why, when man fails us, do we take it out on God?

People's minds or emotions often can't distinguish between men failing them and God, who has nothing to do with people's behavior or failures. Man's failures bring about hurt or offense, which is understandable. Unfortunately, some react to that hurt by quitting and giving up on God in some form or fashion. I don't believe that's understandable. Is it that they don't trust God anymore? Is it that they can't be vulnerable to God anymore? Is it that they can't depend on God like they used to or serve God in the same capacity they used to?

Too many Christians are MIA (missing in action) with God. Too many Christians are deserters in the kingdom of God. Too many Christians are on the injured reserve list. Too many Christians have retired on God. Too many Christians are bitter, mad, critical, and cynical toward God.

Bad things happen in a church. It's a family and it's considered a hospital. There is no reason to take bad occurrences out on God. Get healed, get help, get over it, and engage again. He is the Lord, Master, Ruler, and King in your life, and a man can never be that for you. When you allow man's failures to affect, influence, or stop you from being where God wants you to be or doing what God wants you to do, you have elevated people's influence above God's.

It's terrible to think how many testimonies or stories won't be written or experienced in people's future because people stop on God. People quit on God, gave up on God, and have made things in their life fatal and final by turning in their resignation letters because of man's failures. Who did they take man's failure out on? Who reaps the result of their decision? Who did they blame? Maybe they didn't voice it, but it was seen in their actions. It was Jesus they blamed!

You may cry, get mad, feel disappointed, and be upset, but you're not to take it out on God and blame Him for something man did. In fact, you will never get over the hurt until you are right with God. You will continue to deal with it and may even relive it.

You would never quit a sport because you had a bad coach. You would never end a vocation or career because you had a bad boss. You would never stop eating at a restaurant because you had a bad waiter. You would never stop buying a car because you had a lousy salesperson. Why, then, would we hold a different standard toward God and treat Him worse than those in other areas of our lives?

Cathy Bryant said, "Everything God made was good. Man's the one who messed it up, and we've blamed God for it ever since."

Someone once asked me, after a great fallout at the church I previously attended, how did I not become a part of it or fall victim to it. They also asked why I remained in ministry and moved on from what occurred. I believe they were asking, "How did it not make you bitter?" I responded with three words: "I love God." Seems simple, huh? Not too deep, huh? Profound, huh? Yet, it probably sums up why some do or don't continue in life or with God.

I was once a part of a church where the senior pastor fell into immorality. One week after discovering the news, the church was two-thirds smaller. Now that's probably understandable and may be justifiable.

Here's the tragedy that I've noticed and seen repeatedly. When a pastor fails, like the one involving the church I attended, one-third of the congregation will leave and find another church to plant themselves again in the Body of Christ. One-third of the congregation will remain with the same ministry under new leadership. Unfortunately, they may hear of the incident repeatedly. Sadly, one-third of the congregation will never return to church, period. They left, departed, and said, "No more ever again." Huh?

Does the depth, height, width, and breadth of our love for God matter or make a difference? I think it does. I believe our love for God drives, compels, and motivates. I believe our love for God captivates and restrains us to live a certain way. It's easy to say we love God, but it's much more of a challenge to show God that we love Him, especially considering how we act in challenging times. We can say we love God with words, but how we act when we go through tough times, disappointment, or the unexpected can be a whole different story.

Because I love God, I had to stay with the calling of God on my life, even though others fell. Even though others quit, I had to remain active and available to God in His kingdom. I had to stay in the game and not be on the bench or retire from God's work, even though others gave up.

You're not taking it out on people for what they did or for whatever disappointment you experienced. You're taking it out on God because it's God's calling, mission, and gift that He has given you that you're retiring, deciding never to use again, or won't use to its full potential.

When you say you love God, then love Him by not stopping or giving up because of man's failures. Love Him by continuing, pushing forward, and moving on. When you love God, you won't let what others do stop you from fulfilling your God-given assignment. It may hurt for a while, it may be difficult, and it may not be fun for a time, but don't you quit on God and become decommissioned like a battleship. Stay in the open waters on active duty. Stay in commission, on assignment, going somewhere, and doing something.

Is your love for God or toward God unconditional? I think you would say yes. Then don't make it conditional—only if everything turns out the way you expect, without adversity or disappointment from people. In the words of an old Beatles song, "Get back to where you once belonged." Don't blame God or take circumstances out on God. If you love God, then love Him by re-engaging.

REFLECTION QUESTIONS | The Great Departure

1. When you're hurt, do you ever feel like quitting?

2. Do you think God ought to be blamed for man's failures? Why?

3. How long does it take to re-engage with God after man fails you?

4. What effects could you experience by quitting on God?

5. Are people genuinely better when they stop on God?

Action Item
This week, talk to someone who has left a job, relationship, or church. If they are open to discussing the matter, ask them about their decision.

YOU'RE ONLY AS STRONG AS YOUR PRAYER ALTAR

Every Christian, even many non-Christians, believes prayer is important, but it is often the first to be sacrificed or excused in a busy, hustle-and-bustle life.

Will Rodgers said, "The trouble with our praying is we just do it as a means of last resort."

Augustine said, "On your knees, pray as though it all depends on God. Leave your knees and work as though it all depends on you."

It has also been said, "You stand tallest when you're on your bended knees in prayer."

Questions: Why is it so hard for people to find time to pray? Why is it so hard to be still and focus on prayer? Why are we so easily distracted when we decide to pray? Why do we become good at many things but aren't getting better at prayer? Why do we use prayer only for emergencies, last-minute situations, or desperate measures? Why do we decide on something first or make a commitment to something first, then pray afterward? If I can be blunt, I believe the answer to these questions is simple. The devil hates prayer and will do everything to get us not to pray.

1 Thessalonians 5:17 challenges us always to pray. Jesus, our example, often prayed (Matthew 14:23, Mark 1:35, Luke 9:18, Luke 22:39-41).

Here are some prayer truths that may provide inspiration.

- Prayer invokes God to act and invites God in. It intercepts the devil's activities.
- An acrostic for prayer: **P**raise, **R**epent, **A**sk, **Y**ield.
- Prayer is a declaration of promises found in God's word.
- Prayer qualities: holy, humble, hungry
- Prayer is praying into you everything you need and praying out of you everything you don't like.
- Prayer is praying until the answer comes, not until you get tired.
- Prayer asks God once, then thanks Him for the answer the rest of the time.
- You don't know how to pray all the time, and that's why you need the help of the Holy Spirit.
- Pray before a problem or a need, not after one presents itself.
- Prayers are seeds sown into your future/pathway that you are plowing before you arrive.
- Prayer can't replace or be an excuse for not obeying God's will or word.
- If you hire God, don't fire God with doubt, fear, or unbelief.
- Be excited about prayer as much as God is excited that you are praying.
- You are never so far gone or lost that you can't pray.
- Even when you're not at your best or don't feel like praying,

pray anyway.
- Praying through something is praying consistently every day until there's change; that's called faith.
- Prayer is coming before God's judicial throne room and claiming the rights and privileges that Jesus paid for on Calvary.
- Prayer will take you, in the Spirit, where your flesh won't or can't go.
- Prayer quiets the noise on the outside and brings calmness and quietness to your soul.
- When you wake up, pray. Talk to God before talking to anyone else.
- Prayer is drawing near to God so He can draw near to you.
- Prayer is creating an altar every day and laying everything on it—all your tears, fears, worries, temptations, successes, and decisions.
- Prayer is a wonderful, fresh, new, intimate conversation with your creator, so start talking to Him because He is listening.
- Prayer is understanding that the nature of our flesh is to avoid prayer, so we must fight through doubt, distraction, and discouragement.

Don't be hard on yourself when it comes to prayer. Prayer is not perfect or a performance. It's making an effort to commune with God.

I don't know about you, but I'm not strong enough, fast enough, wise enough, knowledgeable enough, or gifted enough to handle life's successes, failures, heartaches, difficulties, or temptations. I need to pray, and I don't need to pray a little, but much. That's our superpower as Christ-followers. It turns us from Clark Kent to Superman. It's beyond a feeling or emotion; it's a coveted and valued discipline.

REFLECTION QUESTIONS | You're Only As Strong As Your Prayer Altar

1. Are you satisfied with your prayer life?

2. How long can you go without prayer?

3. What are the results when you pray versus when you don't pray?

4. What promises/commitments can you make to God in prayer?

5. Do you share and talk to God about everything or just some things?

Action Item
This week, create an alarm for prayer that's set to go off three times a day. Choose one of those times to pray in silence (no music, TV, or people) as you pray out loud.

INTROVERTED AND DISTANT FROM MY COMMUNITY

Is it a personality thing? Is it an "I don't like people" flaw? Is it a loner/introverted character issue? Is it possible that I like being alone and feel more comfortable by myself than with others or my community? Is it that I've been burned or hurt by people and now shelter to keep others away rather than be hurt again?

We all know we need tribes, packs, community, friends, brothers, and sisters in the family of Jesus Christ. Unfortunately, having and maintaining a relationship may not be a reality for some. There are many people, including me, where superficialness comes much easier than intimacy. Casualness is often easier than personal and intentional. Relationships that allow us to control time, place, expectations, demands, and conversations are preferred over allowing others to be in charge. For some, that may even include Jesus.

We socialize at work and events, and it's a necessity. We fit it on the agenda; it's a need. Anything else can suffer an "I don't want to," "I don't like to," "I don't need to," or "I don't have to" attitude.

There are a lot of people who have a ton of friends, but they may be associates or acquaintances, not close friendships. We have an epidemic of loneliness, depression, and isolation sweeping the land, yet the world's population is growing. How can that be?

Thirty-six percent of Americans deal with loneliness, and sixty-one percent of young adults deal with it. Social distancing, brought about during the COVID-19 Pandemic, and social media have played significant parts in the isolation crisis.

Sharing experiences, stories, hurts, and sins doesn't always come easy for some. Trusting people doesn't come easy, nor does depending on people. Opening up and being transparent is awkward and unnatural for many.

Here's what I know: The longer we isolate, keep our distance, and don't initiate relationships, the simpler not needing them becomes. Also, the more unhealthy we become.

Community protects, comforts, loves, supports, and helps. It works! Will we get hurt? Yes. Will we be disrespected? Yes. However, the gains of a viable friendship far outweigh the emptiness felt by a lonely bedside or a sparsely attended funeral. The Bible tells us that we are better together than alone (Romans 12:4-5).

An Irish proverb states, "A good friend is like a four-leaf clover: hard to find and lucky to get." I was thinking about this the other day as some of my closest friends and confidants have gone to heaven. I felt sad and empty; I may have had a pity party. Then I felt like Jesus challenged me to find and invest in new friends. I thought, *Jesus, it took so long to develop those friendships. They were tested over time, and they proved their loyalty. I could be vulnerable and transparent with them.* Again, I was challenged to find and invest in new friends. "I will show you; I will lead you." That is what I sensed God telling me, and that is what I'm doing now.

Being distant only hurts. One day, you will need someone in your life, or you will suffer more than you should.

When I was young, a bully lived on my street. He approached me one day and told me he would beat me up after school. I asked my friend to go with me to face the bully, and he agreed. It's amazing how less scared I felt with him next to me.

Billy Watterson said, "Things are never quite as scary when you've got a best friend."

Build teams, dream teams, of people that have skills that can help you as you help them. Have cheerleaders, coaches, and counselors. Build relationships like a pyramid, which is narrow at the top. That means you may only have a handful of intimate friendships, and you can tell all your secrets to only a few.

The next level may be friends, and associates are toward the bottom of your pyramid. Associates are not close friends, and you'll have more of them. But here's what I'm saying: Don't be standoffish or skittish. Pursue community, even if it's hard.

The Bible states, "It is not good that man should be alone." That may apply to marriage, but generally, it's also a great principle by which all can live.

REFLECTION QUESTIONS | Introverted and Distant From My Community

1. Are all your friendships at the same level of intimacy?

2. Do you need to do some recruiting for your relationship pyramid?

3. Who are the individuals you identify as having an "intimate friendship" to whom you can tell your secrets?

4. What can you do better to develop lasting friendships?

5. Do you struggle with community? Why?

Action Item
This week, do one thing new with someone you've thought about bringing into your community. Get to know them.

THINGS I'D DO DIFFERENTLY

They say hindsight is 20/20. There's no one who wouldn't do something different if they could, right? We all have regrets about decisions we've made, right? We all wish we had do-overs, right? I believe the answer is yes, but we can't do everything over. We can ask for forgiveness, learn and grow from what took place, and try not to repeat our actions. Additionally, we can help others not to make the mistakes we made.

Max DePree said, "We cannot become what we want to be by remaining what we are."

If, like in golf, I got a mulligan (a do-over), here's how I'd use it. If I had a rewind button, here's how I'd play it. Below is a list of things I would do as I pioneered and built ALFC.

- I would make sure that my family and I were growing together. I grew faster than my spouse because of my responsibility to study, attend meetings and conferences, write books, and mentor others. I didn't always share in her growth by involving her in mine.

- I would accept more invitations to speak at other ministries and bring those relationships and experiences back to my home church. I was too focused on ALFC.

- I would raise a teaching team and more leaders so that the church was not dependent on me and my personality to drive the organization.

- Early on, I would decide what we as a church want to do good and what we will not do, even if the idea is a good thing, and stand by the decisions. I wouldn't allow pressure or distractions to deter me.

- I would slow down and enjoy, reflect, and celebrate with people in a more meaningful way. That would include conversations, affection, or validation.

- I wouldn't be overly concerned about what people think because their acceptance and approval of me often make me hesitate.

- I would try to smile, laugh, and sit more instead of running hard to accomplish goals. I would not allow my responsibilities to change my personality into someone I'm not.

- I would not have as many meetings and make myself unavailable to help solve or fix situations.

- I would think less about attendance and filling seats and more about discipleship, accountability, community, small groups, maturity, and fruitfulness in a believer's life.

- I would not hire out of desperation to fill a position, but I would ensure I select the right person for the job. Although that may delay the ministry's growth, it would eliminate the drama.

- I would listen to the Holy Spirit's leading or my gut rather than be talked into something I don't want to do because of who was asking me to do it.

- I would enjoy better sabbaths with Jesus throughout the week. That way, I can remain refreshed, healthy, and humble to do what I'm asked to do.

- I would have said earlier that it's okay to be me, and I don't have to copy or be someone else. I'm not called to everyone. Everyone won't like me, and that's okay.

- I would try less to control, fix, and change everyone as though that was my responsibility. If people don't want to follow or obey Jesus completely, that is on them.

- I would probably take more chances, take more risks, and be uncomfortable by attempting more.

- I would have celebrated more with others in their victories and successes, especially churches, pastors, and ministries, rather than feel threatened or insecure.

- I would have thought about my retirement, investments, and succession plan earlier.

- I wouldn't take personally people's decision to leave the church. I would remind myself that they aren't mine in the first place.

David Goggins said, "...If you can get through to doing things that you hate to do, on the other side is greatness."

Thank God for Romans 8:1 NLT, which states, "There is no condemnation for those who belong to Christ Jesus."

REFLECTION QUESTIONS | Things I'd Do Differently

1. What does your list of do-overs look like?

2. Where have you changed to do better?

3. Where are you sharing your life experiences with others?

4. Have you forgiven yourself of your mistakes, possessing no guilt?

5. If God gave you more time to live than you think, how would you spend it?

Action Item
Think back, stroll down memory lane, and find a way to redo what you wish you could have done differently.

MANIPULATION, DOMINATION, INTIMIDATION

Edward R. Murrow said, "All I can hope to teach my son is to tell the truth and fear no man."

We are Christ-followers who have taken on a new nature. As the Bible states, we are "a new creation." In Jesus Christ, we should endeavor to live a kind and peaceful life, which is good.

Sometimes, in our striving to show and live goodness out, we can have unfiltered, unconditional, blind loyalty to people. The Bible challenges us to believe the best of every person's intention, but not all people have the right intentions, motives, and hearts.

Sometimes, in our blind loyalty or naivety, we fall victim to people's schemes, shenanigans, or games. Be on guard and watchful for these people in and outside the church—Christians and non-Christians, saved and unsaved, humans and animals (just kidding).

Some people tend to manipulate, dominate, and intimidate others. These people are not of God, no matter what they say or their position or title. You have a God-conscience and a will that should never be manipulated.

Whenever and wherever there is the practice of this trio—manipulation, domination, and intimidation—there is the presence of witchcraft because that is how the devil runs his kingdom. It's done through manipulation, domination, and intimidation. The devil controls, threatens, lies, deceives, represses, forces subjection, terrorizes, and bullies. There is no motive of love in him. In our blind Christian loyalty, we can fall victim to this environment.

People who want to control other people have issues. When they influence others, they think it makes them confident, respected, and more prominent than they are. This type of individual loves to make people feel threatened by them. They want others to feel as if they can do something to them, but they can't if others don't allow it. They can be disarmed.

There is a person in the Bible named Jezebel who operated under this spirit. She used manipulation, domination, and intimidation to rule her kingdom. She even influenced and affected the great prophet Elijah, paralyzing his gifts. He was full of fear, felt threatened, and behaved irrationally.

I've worked in an environment where the boss made everyone fearful. Everyone walked on eggshells hoping not to tick off the boss. Needless to say, there was no peace in that environment.

Beware of the following situations:

- You're being made to do something that violates scripture or your conscience.
- Someone makes themselves seem more spiritual than you, throwing around their title or giftedness to lord it over you.
- Someone scares you or threatens your welfare or well-being.

- You need someone's permission to do things they have no authority to tell you not to do.

- Someone seeks to know everything about you and control your life.

- Someone stretches the truth to make themselves look good, and won't tell the whole truth about a matter.

- Someone never repents of the wrong they've done, and always wants to look good in people's eyes.

- Someone makes you feel bad because you don't agree with them or see things the way they see things.

- Someone makes you think you cannot live or thrive without them or outside of them.

- You are asked to be the fall guy or front person for someone else's decision or asked to do something that someone else should be doing. You know it is wrong or you feel uncomfortable.

How many times in the Bible does it say, "Fear not"? It's stated 365 times, one for every day of the year. Matthew 10 tells us to fear God and never fear man.

Don't be manipulated, dominated, or intimidated by a pastor, board, top giver, church member, someone calling themselves by a spiritual title, mate, child, or the devil. God is love, and love casts out all fear.

REFLECTION QUESTIONS | Manipulation, Domination, Intimidation

1. Have you ever experienced this trio in your life?

2. How does being manipulated, dominated, and intimidated make you feel?

3. How do you respond to this trio?

4. Is there anything in your life causing you to operate in this trio?

5. How can you oppose this trio today? What will you begin to do?

Action Item
This week, initiate a conversation with someone who intimidates you. Confront your anxiety and ask them at least three questions to get to know them.

TOO CONFOUNDING AND PERPLEXING FOR ME

Mark Twain said, "It is better to keep your mouth closed and let people think you are a fool than to open it and remove all doubt."

Proverbs 17:28 AMPC states, "Even a fool when he holds his peace is considered wise; when he closes his lips he is esteemed a man of understanding."

You and I know people who have opinions about everything or have figured out everything in this world. So many are experts on all the troubles and drama in politics, education, healthcare, and social issues, in addition to people's personal lives.

Can any man or woman know everything about everything or everyone? No! Only God truly knows for sure.

Many people are theorists, skeptics, critics, thinkists, and interpretists. (I made up the last two words, but you know what I'm saying.) Some people get way too upset or angry about things they may not know the truth about.

Is the news always accurate? Is social media always accurate? Is what anyone says always accurate? Are your emotions always authentic? No!

I love the scripture by King David in Psalm 131:1-2 NLT, "LORD, my heart is not proud; my eyes are not haughty. I don't concern myself with matters too great or too awesome to grasp. Instead, I have calmed and quieted myself like a weaned child who no longer cries for its mother's milk. Yes, like a weaned child is my soul within me."

Have you heard the statement, "That is above my pay grade"? David experienced a lot of things he couldn't figure out completely. He took the approach: "I won't and don't concern myself with stuff I can't grasp—matters that are difficult for me to understand the ins and outs of or the why, when, and where of life." David would say, "I've learned to quiet and calm myself down and trust God who knows the truth, the why, and the solutions to all matters."

David faced a father-in-law who was trying to kill him. He had friends who turned their backs on him. He was in a marriage that didn't work out. He experienced many issues involving his children, as well as employees who didn't follow his orders, and the list goes on.

"I don't know, but God knows" is probably a good response for people who want to know your opinion or desire to bait you into a conversation that may reveal your ignorance or stir up your anger. God has figured it all out, so that may mean you don't have to.

There are many facts we know and can confidently communicate our stance or opinion; however, for things that we only know in part or have little experience with, we should think twice before putting down the gauntlet by saying, "I know some things for sure." Be on guard and exhibit self-awareness toward things that are productive, unproductive, helpful, unhelpful, healthy, unhealthy, good, bad, beneficial, and unbeneficial to you and for you.

I have a friend who is a Greek scholar of the New Testament. I asked him a question, and without hesitation, he said, "I don't know the answer to that." Wow! It shocked me that his pride and humility were displayed when he said, "I don't know…." That was brilliant!

I know that a lot of time can be spent and emotion expressed concerning things that I probably can't change, don't have anything to do with me, or may have already occurred. Why people do what they do, why things don't work out as they should, and why situations occurred that I thought shouldn't have is too perplexing. God knows, and I will trust God and leave it in His hands.

I had a friend who built a hospital, but it went bankrupt. When I asked him how he felt about that, he said, "It hurt, but I can't always explain the answer to why things work out and why, sometimes, they don't." Brilliant!

REFLECTION QUESTIONS | Too Confounding and Perplexing For Me

1. Are you quick to give your opinion about everything?

2. Have you ever thought something was true only to find out differently?

3. Can certain issues stir up emotions and take you to unhealthy places?

4. Do you speak about things from the viewpoint of expertise or speculation?

5. Can you walk away from a conversation you don't know the absolute truth about?

Action Item
This week, spend quality time with someone who is better than you at a particular skill. Use this as a time of discovery. Ask them about the process that went into developing the skill.

THE TRIO OF TEMPTATIONS

Jesus was tempted three times in the wilderness by the devil. Adam and Eve were tempted in the Garden of Eden by the devil. Delilah seduced Samson. Potiphar's wife enticed Joseph to sleep with her. The devil persuaded Judas to betray Jesus. No one is exempt from temptation, but we don't have to be victims or succumb to temptation.

C.S. Lewis said, "A man who gives in to temptation after five minutes simply does not know what it would have been like an hour later."

Temptation comes in all forms and fashions to each of us, and we don't always have a bent toward the same attractions. Some are tempted by desserts, but some aren't. Some are tempted to lie when some won't. I think you get the picture. Some temptations are stronger and more damaging than others. Some temptations reap greater consequences and repercussions than others.

In Matthew 4:1, we read that the devil tempted Jesus in three familiar areas. I first heard a message on the subject taught by a preacher named Robby Gallaty, which enlightened me. Here's what we learn from these temptations.

1. Bread: This can represent appetites. "Do I have enough?"
2. "If you are the Son of God:" This can represent approval. "Am I being enough?"
3. Kingdom of this world: This can represent ambition. "Am I doing enough?"

This trio of temptations can be viewed as a pattern or categories that the devil will use on us all, and they often lead people astray. This trio, like a predator with its prey, snares or traps its victims. As a result, people don't fulfill their God-given purpose, which causes heartache, pain, embarrassment, and destruction.

One time, a rat got into my truck's engine and ate a bunch of electrical wiring, which caused hundreds of dollars in damage. I tried various things to keep it out, but it kept coming back, or at least its family did. Someone told me dryer sheets would keep it away, so I tried it. Guess what? I had no more rats creeping or sneaking into my truck. I, eventually, closed the door against the rat, and that's how we deal with temptation; close the entry point.

Allow me to be vulnerable for a moment to help others express what's real about their temptations. Let's consider my life and ministry.

Regarding the first area of temptation, my appetite wasn't and isn't for food, money, or material possessions. My appetite is toward the beauty of a woman, and it's something I must guard myself against. Lust and imagination can become real to me in the wrong way. The Bible talks about the lust of the eyes. That may look like a long stare, focusing on a loosely dressed woman wearing revealing clothing. That's especially likely when it comes to television. There may be nudity, and that image can remain in my mind like a digital imprint.

Approval, for me, isn't so much wanting to hear it or be liked, even though everyone desires some form of affirmation. For me, it can look like impatience that may turn into frustration. Frustration can lead to moments of anger or outbursts. I may become impatient because of how long something is taking; how slow people can sometimes be. That includes how people drive, walk, and talk.

Regarding ambition, there's a competitive nature within me that may become a bit envious of others' success, opportunities, or privileges in ministry. The envy causes me to think I am less than them and they are greater than me, or I simply want what they have.

In my life, I must lay this trio on the altar of God every day. I must monitor my behavior, be extremely aware, and, on occasion, make myself accountable to others. I can't play ignorant with this trio. They aren't new foes; they are old foes who have tried, many times, to trap me and make me a victim.

What are your temptations related to appetite, approval, and ambition? Do you ask yourself, "Do I have enough, am I good enough, or am I doing enough?"

Know that being honest and transparent doesn't show weakness. I believe it shows courage, humility, and strength. It's choosing not to give any place to the devil (Ephesians 4:27).

Arnold Glasow said, "Temptation usually comes in through a door that has deliberately been left open."

REFLECTION QUESTIONS | The Trio of Temptations

1. Can you name your temptations related to the trio of appetite, approval, and ambition?

2. Share where you have fallen victim to the trio.

3. What do you do to protect yourself from the trio?

4. Do you consider this trio to be damaging?

5. To kill this trio, what would your altar of sacrifice look like?

Action Item
Go to one of your accountability partners and share your most recent temptation and how you avoided the temptation.

INTEGRITY AND IMAGE

Image can be how people perceive you. Integrity can be how God perceives you. Image can be trying to look a certain way in front of people to impress them. Integrity can be trying to look good in God's eyes.

People, especially leaders, can be driven by image. Image can involve a particular look or way of dressing. It can involve a way of talking. It can involve a way of posing, like by a vehicle, house, or with jewelry. Image can involve bragging about who you know, where you've been, or what you've done to gain acceptance or create followers.

Image can be driven by platforms or the marketing of self for selfish gain. It's popular in the selling of self and seems acceptable in all facets of life. The term "image" has become a trendy catchphrase for branding.

We live in a world where everyone talks and brags about themselves. Integrity, however, doesn't talk; it shows it and lives it. Remember, your lifestyle speaks louder than your words.

It has been said, "Image requires advertising. Integrity needs no advertising; it speaks for itself."

Integrity is who you are, no matter who sees you. It's who you are when no one is looking at you. Integrity is seen in how you handle money, anger, and sexual matters. It's the ethics and morals that you hold to. I call it the non-negotiables. Non-negotiables say, "No matter what, I won't _____ " (you fill in the blank). Non-negotiables say, "I won't lie, I won't cheat, I won't compromise, I won't quit, I won't exaggerate, I won't touch something, I won't watch something, I won't listen to something."

People are always trying to stand out, distinguish themselves, draw attention to themselves, be noticed, or gain the admiration and applause of others. They want to awe and impress others with their looks, smarts, giftedness, talents, abilities, positions, and titles. That is all image-driven, which can pump up one's ego and starve one's humility.

I strive to be a nobody, inconspicuous, invisible, and anonymous. The Bible speaks of this in 1 Corinthians 15:9 and Ephesians 3:8. In the words of John the Baptist about Jesus, "He must increase, but I must decrease" (John 3:30). That's probably a good statement to live by.

In life, everything wants to tell you, "You're the man," "You're a diva," or "You're the goat (greatest of all time)." Everything in Hollywood is about award shows or The Walk of Fame. They even have image awards. I want to push people toward Jesus. It's because of Him, and Him alone, that I can do what I do. He is the gift giver, blesser, grace giver, and promoter, not me or you. As the Bible reveals, there is nothing good in us outside of Christ (Romans 7:18). I am nothing; He is everything!

Integrity lives by a higher standard of not trying to get away with anything. It doesn't use shortcuts. It's living a blameless, harmless life without fraud, hypocrisy, or deceit. It's living in honesty and truthfulness. Integrity has a sensitive conscience and knows wrong, error, dishonesty, and falsehood. It does not incline to avoid what's right.

Integrity will keep its promises, take responsibility for its actions, and remember its obligations. Integrity cares more about what looks good on the inside than the outside; however, image is primarily concerned with the outward appearance.

In the world of social media, we must guard against the allure of trying to look good—selfie this, post that. Is it all bad? No. But checking one's attitude, motives, and reasons are important.

Social media can be deceptive. Generally, we see edited versions of people's lives; flaws, failures, and mistakes are often left out or distorted.

One of the greatest compliments someone gave me when they were talking to me, having no idea who I was, "Wow! I didn't know you were the pastor of this great church."

One day, Jesus rode a donkey into Jerusalem where people were celebrating. They were shouting, "Hosanna." The streets were lined with people engaged in a parade of loud cheers. Who was the attention on, Jesus or the donkey? I think you know the answer.

Don't be confused, and don't be the hee-hawing donkey (ass) that thinks it's all about you.

REFLECTION QUESTIONS | Integrity and Image

1. Where can you be a victim of too much image because of what you do?

2. What does image look like to you?

3. What does integrity look like to you?

4. What are you overly confident and braggadocios about?

5. Who gets the glory and honor in your life? Does your attitude reflect that?

Action Item
Purchase a Starbucks menu item (or any restaurant item) for a stranger this week.

GROUNDED

People can easily fall into the latest fads and trends. People can easily be influenced by hype and emotions and easily get caught up in leisure and pleasure. People can quickly become displeased with possessions (things) and people.

Grounded is maintaining a clear perspective about everything and not just seeing things from your viewpoint. In other words, I may be experiencing good things in my life, but I realize others aren't. I may have many liberties and freedoms, but I recognize that others don't. I may have good health, marriage, kids, friendships, money, and material blessings, but I acknowledge some don't have these things.

Being grounded is remaining grateful, sensitive, compassionate, generous, helpful, and prayerful without forgetting who provided for you. It's purposefully remembering that some don't have and may never have your experiences, privileges, and opportunities. It's also realizing that you haven't always had them. You're not better, smarter, wiser, more gifted, or loved by God because you have what others don't.

After I finish a long weekend of preaching sermons, sometimes I like to walk by myself to my car to stay grounded and tell Jesus,

"Thank you." Sometimes, before I speak from someone else's platform, I go to a bathroom, get on one knee, and thank God for the opportunity. Before I go to bed at night, I kneel and give God thanks. Sometimes, I drive around my church and thank Jesus for using me and blessing me with the opportunity I've been given. I don't want to take anything for granted. I want everything to remain a privilege and honor. That's being grounded.

Being grounded is possessing a good head and a clear perspective, focus, and reference point in life. It should be preferred over doing no reality check and not recognizing the real hardships in the world. Having an understanding heart is what it's all about.

There are Christians living in challenging and harsh conditions worldwide with little to no luxuries or conveniences. Some people and churches put their lives and ministries at risk in countries that persecute them for believing in Jesus. I want to remember that.

Hebrews 13:3 states, "Remember the prisoners as if chained with them—those who are mistreated—since you yourselves are in the body also."

I want to force myself, amid all my blessings, not to take anything for granted but to remember those in chains. That may be prison chains, chains of abuse and misuse, chains of poverty, chains of loneliness, chains of loss/death, chains of slavery, chains of mental or emotional bondage, chains of addiction or obsession, chains of shame, or chains of guilt and sin.

Constant awareness and interest in people's struggles should cause us to consider our impact on our communities. It should provoke us to ask, "What good am I doing or withholding?" It should cause us to examine our attitudes and actions, which keep us grounded.

Grounded is remaining compassionate and empathetic to people's struggles, plights, problems, and difficulties. Grounded is to see life through other people's lenses. There's an adage that states, "Don't judge someone until you've walked a mile in their shoes." That doesn't mean we excuse the actions of others, but we put in context what they have been through.

There is something in the health world called living or being grounded. It has to do with the science of walking barefoot upon the earth with the electric heating properties that God created charging our bodies. I think there's a message in there for us.

Let's remember those that don't have and not think we're better because we do.

REFLECTION QUESTIONS | Grounded

1. How do you stay grounded?

2. Do you let the things in your life puff you up?

3. Are there individuals struggling in life that you are helping?

4. How do you live a grateful life?

5. Can you say "thank you" more to people?

<u>Action Item</u>
Help someone outside your home (work, school, interest group, etc.) with a task. Tell them, "Thank you for allowing me to help."

ADRENALINE LAWS

In ministry work, preaching, and leading a business, there are a ton of adrenaline rushes, thrills, or highs. If I can be blunt, adrenaline is addicting. We desire applause, accomplishments, opportunities, victories, status, recognition, platforms, and audiences.

In ministry, the highs are felt from one song to the next, from one sermon to the next, from one Easter/Super Bowl to the next, from one campus to another, from one salvation, testimony, and miracle to another, from one successful counseling session, wedding, or funeral to the next, from one good offering to a good stewardship campaign, from the acquisition of a new building to the next structure. You get the picture.

In the business world, the highs are felt from one paycheck, commission, or bonus to the next, from one client or contract signing to the next, and one competition or award presentation to the next.

Highs are pure excitement. It's a feeling of "I'm needed, I'm wanted, I'm important, I'm asked for."

Raphael Saadiq said, "It's the adrenaline rush you only get from being in front of an audience. It's addictive."

When the body experiences challenges and stress, there is a release of adrenaline. It helps individuals focus so that they can take on the situation. It's what an athlete feels during a competition. It's the sensation experienced by a skydiver or bungee jumper; it's exuberating. Like being on a roller coaster as it descends and twists, it will amp you up, or in the words of Arnold Schwarzenegger, "It will pump you up" (please say it with the accent).

Nigel Mansell said, "I've tried everything other than jumping out of a plane, but nothing gives you an adrenaline rush like racing a car."

Highs, however, don't last. The adrenaline can't last. The pure exuberance won't remain. The amps shouldn't last. Downshifting, like in automobiles, is necessary to sustain a healthy, long-term existence. These can be called recovery periods. It's when rest, relaxation, and calmness occur to lower the heart rate. It can be described as a strategy, reset, or reboot in your emotions. You need it in order to engage in the next challenge, excitement, or draining situation. This could look like starting from first gear or coming to a complete stop before you rev the engine, stir up the RPMs, and race again to fifth gear at 100 miles per hour.

Sports doctors, when studying athletes, are not just looking at how high the heart rate can become or what the athlete can produce. They are also focused on how quickly, when they stop, the heart rate returns to a normal state or how long it takes the individual to stop breathing heavily.

I think living on adrenaline or moving fast all the time can lead to burnout, fatigue, frustration, low productivity, misplaced priorities, joyless living, and not truly appreciating the journey. It's difficult to enjoy the journey if the ride is too fast to notice the beauty of things.

I went on a trip to Maryland to attend a pastor's conference once with my wife Cindy. It was our first East Coast trip. We had a three-hour window between sessions at one point during the conference. Cindy and I decided to take a train into Washington, DC, to take in the sights. By the time we arrived, we had only 45 minutes to spend there before we had to head back to the conference. I asked a taxi driver to take us to as many historical locations as he could in that brief segment of time. We raced by the White House, Washington Monument, Lincoln Memorial, Smithsonian, and Vietnam Memorial.

To be honest, it's all a blur because everything happened so fast. I don't remember any of it, and I can't appreciate what I saw because I was trying to accomplish too much too fast on adrenaline instead of slowing down.

Bode Miller said, "A huge adrenaline rush is usually followed by a pretty low point."

You will experience adrenaline rushes but make sure you come back down. Take time to park, breathe, and put yourself in first gear again. Cool the engine and take a long breath; inhale and exhale.

In the Bible, many of the Psalms end with the word "Selah." It's stated 75 times (see Psalm 3:8, Psalm 24:10). It means to pause, to be silent from the singing or the performance. It can also signify an intermission. I love that description. We should apply it in our lives. We don't have to be quick to move on to the next performance. We can have "selah" moments to catch our breath.

REFLECTION QUESTIONS | Adrenaline Laws

1. Do you have any adrenaline rushes in your life?

2. What gives you an adrenaline rush?

3. Have you experienced the negative side of adrenaline rushes?

4. What would a "selah" moment look like to you?

5. Do you love adrenaline rushes more than pauses, or prefer pauses over adrenaline rushes?

Action Item
Do something that takes you out of your comfort zone. Afterward, tell someone how it made you feel.

MORE MEANS MORE

Forgive my naivety. Forgive my ignorance. Forgive my stupidity. Forgive the innocence of my early career. We preachers, like everyone else, just want more to happen. We want more audiences, more influence, more followers, more members, more notoriety, more income, more opportunities, more platforms, and more invitations. But here is the truth that I learned: More means more.

It's not just the substance or increase that comes, but more time is needed, more energy is needed, more opinions are given, more responsibility comes, more expectations, more sacrifices, more criticism, more loneliness, more temptations, more tiredness, and much more that escapes predictability.

You've likely heard the phrase, "It's not all it's cracked up to be." I should have prayed to God, concerning the more, to give me the capacity to handle the more. I should have asked Him to provide me with strength, wisdom, humility, and grace to handle the more.

Two scriptures in the Bible talk to me about this topic. The first, "For everyone to whom much is given, from him much will be required" (Luke 12:48), and the second, "…Count the cost" (Luke 14:28), which is what we should do before we decide anything.

More is like a coin, which has two sides. One side of the coin represents the liberty, freedom, rights, and privileges you obtain. The other side of the coin represents the burdens and heaviness that come with the other side.

Specifically, in my church, more people has meant more people get sick, die, divorce, lose jobs, and relocate. There are more teenage issues. More leave the church because of offense. We facilitate more funerals and counseling sessions. All of this can take a toll on you and wear on the soul. I've heard it said, "Higher levels, higher devils."

I've had to hire more staff to help me facilitate the people—children, youth, marriages, elderly, and everything in between—and that comes with a cost. That means more money—higher budget/payroll—and a human resources department.

Another more is more buildings and vision, and that has required more asking, fundraising, offerings, and campaigns. More exposure has caused less privacy, seclusion, and being able to go somewhere incognito.

More starts off glamorous, exciting, fun, alluring, and attractive as it glistens in the sun. I don't want to say it's like pyrite (fake gold), but the glisten does fade after a while, especially when wisdom steps in, perspectives change, and maturity arises, which are needed.

I believe that what's been required of me with the more is more prayer, and with more prayer has come more faith, trust, and dependence. I rely more on God, and, more and more, I understand that I can't handle more without Him. I can't be more without Him. I can't have more without Him.

More has required more brokenness, emptiness, and nothingness from me, which produces humility, appreciation, generosity, and compassion for all that has been loaned to me, whatever that is or will be.

More isn't all it's cracked up to be. It's like someone who starts collecting stuff. At some point, they realize they have nowhere to put the growing collection. The items begin taking over the living space. At some point, the collection is moved into the garage and eventually a storage unit (hopefully, you get what I'm saying). It starts small and, if not managed well, thought through, and prayed through, it can take over and turn into disappointment.

REFLECTION QUESTIONS | More Means More

1. What have both sides of the "more" coin looked like for you?

2. How can you better prepare for more?

3. Can more be an advantage or disadvantage?

4. Describe your more. What do you want more of?

5. What are you willing to risk to acquire more?

Action Item
Learn a coworker's, team member's, or classmate's task, and ask how you can assist them.

STIFLE GROWTH

Whether in a church, business, marriage, or one's personal life, it can happen—growth can be stifled.

Genesis 1:28 states, "Then God blessed them, and God said to them, 'Be fruitful and multiply; fill the earth and subdue it; have dominion....'"

I know there's a grace gift on the mega-church (2000+). I recognize that most churches (98%) are less than 200 people, and most prefer to attend a small church of 200 people or less.

People have always asked me if I knew or sensed that ALFC (the church I pastor) would be a mega-church. My answer is "No." I did not know ALFC would be a mega-church. However, there are a few things I did besides praying, preaching, exercising integrity, loving people, and having a desire for ministry, which we call basic skills or understanding.

I've always thought big. That's not in comparison to other churches but to malls, restaurants, companies, beaches, neighborhoods, and communities. I thought, *If they are not having a hard time attracting people, why should we?* It didn't matter if we were in my house, a school, renting a suite in a business park, or hosting services in our 4000-seat auditorium. I always saw it filled with people, not empty.

Being a visionary has always been important to me—to be ahead of the people I was trying to inspire. It was about showing and telling them where we were going next, and it was all for the glory of God. That included a vision for orphanages, the lost, a vision for campuses/expansion, the needy, the sick, the incarcerated, single mothers, widows, the disabled, the poor, and the homeless. Vision for marriages, financial freedom, health education, and overcoming classes were as important.

Here's the thought: Wherever God has placed a church in a community, there are needs. Find out what those needs are and make a difference in the community you are called to.

I was never intimidated by people's gifts, whether they were volunteers, board members, or staff. I never competed with them, stifled them, or feared them by taking control. I wanted the church to grow, and I needed others' gifts to do that. That meant I had to delegate opportunities and responsibilities to others to have the freedom to dream and cast a vision. Doing so allowed people to develop and soar.

I constantly challenge my staff with the statement, "I don't pay you to do but reproduce." They are to teach people, mentor, bring people alongside them, and work their way out of a job. In doing so, they become more valuable to me, and by this, they will always have a job. "Don't mother hen a job or ministry" was a phrase I used (sort of speak).

Ralph B. Perry said, "Ignorance deprives people of freedom because they do not know what alternatives there are. It is impossible to choose to do what one has never heard of."

I never felt the need to micro-manage others. I trusted the people I hired and let them make the necessary decisions. Correction took place whenever necessary, but I didn't feel the need to know everything. I would say, "I'm the general practitioner on staff; you are the experts or specialists in your fields." Not having the need to hear from me all the time was a good sign, and it allowed me to macro-manage and observe from a distance. It's not that I didn't know what was going on, but I endeavored to train and cross-train well. It's what we did and still do. Preparation, strategy, follow-up, and employees being ready are critically important.

Next, having volunteers, staff, and leaders align with the ministry's vision, mission, goals, and objectives was imperative for clarity, sacrifice, and unity. I'm always trying to give understanding so that no one feels left out or in the dark about crucial information. I want them to know what we've done or what lies ahead in the future. Additionally, we show appreciation to the volunteers with a celebration dinner, T-shirts, resources, praise, and thank yous.

We should continuously improve, which may include self-evaluations, critical thinking, learning from others, and secret shoppers/visitors. These things challenge us to do our best.

Whenever my team came before me and was asked if they were ready, they had to be. Nothing loosey-goosey, shabby, or of less than excellent quality and efficiency was acceptable.

Thoughtful services where everything is thought out, purposeful, meaningful, relatable, and understandable to reach those who have never been to church and the seasoned churchgoer is important. We've always thought out our altar calls—what we say, how we do them, how we want people to respond, and what we want them to do next. We never overlook this precious invitation. Additionally, it's important to have a quality of excellence in music, songs, language, announcements, offerings, preaching, activities, and events.

The building's look, smell, and atmosphere are also important. A large structure was needed to handle large altar calls, packed new member classes, major counseling issues, huge events, sizeable services, and numerous problems and crises. There is a difference between small mindsets (mom and pop) and big mindsets (multitudes).

Additionally, the financial integrity of a budget to run the ministry with percentages and margins is essential. A percentage is designated toward payroll, mortgage, savings, administrative costs, and missions. Sticking and staying with that budget is crucial. I have never been shy about presenting to the church annually to show them where the money was going.

I'm also adamant about raising up a leadership culture. These individuals are developed through leadership courses. Doing so aids us in preparing the next generation of hires, department leaders, elders, deacons, or marketplace leaders. It has been our bullpen of leaders from which we can quickly and easily select.

Lastly, I've never made a promise to people that I didn't keep. If I said it in the pulpit, I must follow through. Reputation and trust are high values. Furthermore, I never allowed gimmicks, fads, trends, or extremism related to money and preaching. I avoid long and tiring services, meetings, and guest speakers.

These practices have served me well.

REFLECTION QUESTIONS | Stifle Growth

1. What do you do well, and what don't you do well?

2. What is your greatest struggle in ministry, business, or your personal life?

3. Where can you start to change or do things differently?

4. Is there anything that does not run timely?

5. Is there anything that is not orderly?

Action Item
Write down a project that seems too big for you. Share that idea with someone in your accountability circle. It can be a new system or an event you have had on your heart, but you feel it is out of reach.

CLEAN = UNUSED, DIRTY = USED

Proverbs 14:4 TPT states, "The only clean stable is an empty stable. So if you want the work of an ox and to enjoy an abundant harvest, you'll have a mess or two to clean up!"

There's nothing wrong with tidiness, cleanliness, orderliness, spotlessness, or a desire to be immaculate, but not at the expense of something or someone, or as a reason for something not to be used, worn, or inhabited.

Boats are meant to sail the ocean. That means they are intended to be used, not docked, not washed and waxed every day. They get mossy and attract barnacles.

Most cars are to be driven on the open road. That means parts of the vehicle will become worn, scratched, or dented. Vehicles aren't meant to sit in garages to be admired, at least not the average car.

Shoes are to be worn. They cover your feet as you walk from one destination to another. They're not meant to sit in pristine condition in a closet doing nothing. They're meant to get dirty and scuffed.

I like getting sweaty, literally and symbolically. I like the challenge of attempting and doing something, not just talking about it and wishing for something to happen. I love experimenting with communication styles, reaching children and youth with new adventures. I like changing music styles to appeal to different people than we usually reach. It may make some a bit uncomfortable, but it results in lives being committed to the faith.

George S. Patton Jr. said, "An active mind cannot exist in an inactive body."

A few years ago, we hosted youth outreaches on church grounds. The events attracted kids who would typically never come to church but came for these events. They arrived just as they were—in appearance, talk, and habits. Over time, the property became stained with graffiti. I heard that people were getting upset over what had been done and the inconvenience of cleaning up graffiti. I remember laughing and feeling glad about being tagged. I told those who were upset, "It's only going to cost us some paint to restore the walls. We built the church for those individuals too, not just us."

Some people want to control everything, organize everything, and dictate everything. What price, though, can we put on those teenagers that heard about Jesus?

It's okay to get messy and dirty because we're reaching lost people, helping hurting people, and attracting different people. So what if the pillows get thrown onto the ground, cups fall to the floor, and fingerprints appear on the walls if someone had a good time and something great occurred in their lives. It means something was used, enjoyed, liked, or attended. Messiness and noise are signs of something happening, and that's better than everything being quiet, reserved, and unchanged.

When my grandchildren come to the house and feel comfortable enough to kick off their shoes, open the refrigerator, and touch items in the house, that's cool to me.

To reach people, help people, touch people, and love people, let's get messy by experimenting—attempting something we've never done before. Let's get messy by forging new reputations, experiences, and stories to share.

Sometimes, like a beverage, you have to shake something before you partake because some ingredients settle and become separate. It sat too long in an inactive state. The ingredients are revived for optimum taste or production when it's shaken. So it is in life.

What happens to a body that's been in bed too long? It breaks down. No one wants that outcome.

Jack LaLanne said, "So many older people, they just sit around all day long and they don't get any exercise. Their muscles atrophy, and they lose their strength, their energy and vitality by inactivity."

Let's get doing, let's get moving, let's get active.

REFLECTION QUESTIONS | Clean = Unused, Dirty = Used

1. What new things are you willing to try?

2. What would getting messy look like to you?

3. Where do you need to be more active?

4. Is it okay to try new things and leave the outcome out of the equation?

5. If you reach out to challenging/difficult people, what will happen?

Action Item
Select a skill you recently learned and work on improving that skill.

relatio
point o
Think
the mi
withou
To ho

PRACTICAL WISDOM

Proverbs 19:8 states, "He who gets wisdom loves his own soul; He who keeps understanding will find good."

Proverbs 4:5-6 states, "Get wisdom! Get understanding! Do not forget, nor turn away from the words of my mouth. Do not forsake her, and she will preserve you; Love her, and she will keep you."

Prior to establishing our church, I was an assistant pastor (1985 to 1994) earning a full-time salary. When we formed our church in 1994 with twelve people in our home, I continued to work for eighteen months at two secular jobs. I was employed as a warehouse worker earning minimum wage. Although I was a pastor, I couldn't go into full-time ministry with a full-time salary.

Because our small church couldn't afford to pay me, I didn't take a salary to avoid being a financial burden on our young, fledgling church. We had to save money, pay rent on a public school campus, purchase sound equipment, and manage other expenses (stationery, children's curriculum, etc.). Our top priority was not figuring out how to pay a pastor's salary. Putting the church's needs first was our objective. We could have drained that little church of its finances, but that would not have been good stewardship. I was young, strong, and capable of working to provide for my family, so I chose to be bi-vocational.

Over the years, I've seen ministers start churches, and people start businesses who didn't want to work a secular job to help get the organization off the ground. They didn't want to work two jobs until the new endeavor could afford to pay them. I've seen many young pastors who wouldn't work, and they expected their young church to pay them a salary. I don't know if that's faith or foolishness. I lean toward the latter.

Voltaire said, "Common sense is not so common."

Sometimes, ego, pride, or laziness can play a part in why a pastor would take a salary when the church can't afford it. They can use that money in better ways to help the church succeed. The same is true for a business venture.

Samuel Taylor Coleridge said, "Common sense in an uncommon degree is what the world calls wisdom." I call it plain hard work.

I think God honors faithfulness, good stewardship, ethics, and integrity. When a pastor or leader puts the needs of the church, customer, or family in front of his own, that opens the door for testimonies and incredible stories of trusting God.

It's amazing how God graced me in those early years to work the third shift at a warehouse, sometimes a double shift. He graced me to be a husband and father and do all the work required to lead a growing church. It wasn't easy, but it was rewarding.

I never wanted to abuse or misuse the church finances. I decided to model to our congregation what our true motives were and to be an example without reproach. It was also an opportunity to show God the sincerity of our hearts. God always showed up and helped me with the early cares and burdens of starting a church, working a job, and caring for my family.

If you work hard in the beginning, sacrifice where and when necessary, and do what it takes to succeed, you can reap the benefits in the years to come. But if you refuse to work hard in the beginning, you may not make it.

I believe practicing good common sense rather than wishful thinking reaps great results. I believe good common sense can help us avoid unnecessary frustrations and disappointments. I believe good common sense takes the guesswork out of most circumstances.

Knowing what needs to be done first before what you do second, knowing one has to be a good steward over the little before he can have bigger, knowing what you have to do now before there can be a next, and knowing where first base is before thinking about home plate is essential.

Common sense and practicality may look like buying used before buying new. Knowing what you can and can't afford is common sense. Saving before spending is common sense. Preparing, planning, and strategizing before you execute is common sense. Researching, examining, and evaluating is common sense.

REFLECTION QUESTIONS | Practical Wisdom

1. Is there a practical side to dreaming?

2. What does hard work and sacrifice produce?

3. If someone won't work to acquire their dreams, what would you call that?

4. Should you leave a secure job/income to start a new venture when there's no other income to depend on?

5. What are the steps to starting a business venture?

Action Item
Write what you've learned so far from this book. Advance on a new idea this week using the knowledge you've gained. Additionally, list any ideas you must now reconsider.

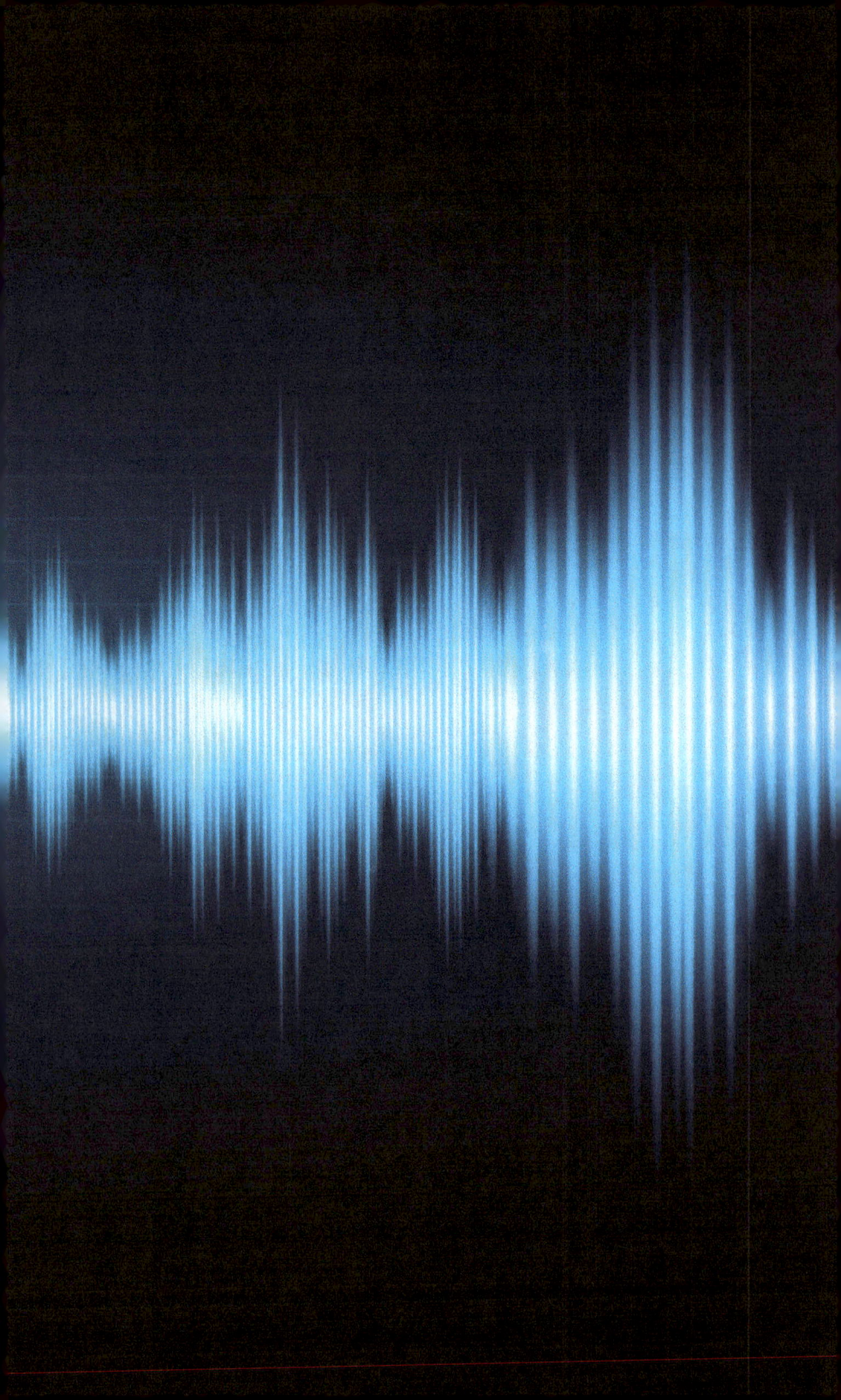

ACCEPTABLE NOISE LEVEL

To the listener, a radio, TV, movie theater, concert, airplane, motorcycle, and public event have an acceptable noise level. Even in the library, there is an acceptable noise level.

What is your tolerable, acceptable noise level? Some people need silence, no movement, and no noise to perform.

Life is filled with noises, chatter, clanging, and shouting. It's like a basketball, baseball, or football game with cheers, boos, clapping, sneers, singing, yelling, name-calling, and much more. Life is unlike a golf game where the golfer requires absolute silence to hit the golf ball.

Having raised three sons in our home, I couldn't always ask for or expect silence. I had to study, read, and write sermons amid the noise. There were no noise-cancelling headphones back then. I may have been in another room, but in our apartment or 970 sq. ft. home, where you still can hear the sound, I had to learn to concentrate amid the noise level. I had to listen to what was going on and hear, through other sounds, to determine if it was acceptable noise, like kids playing, or unacceptable noise, like someone getting hurt.

There will always be noise from critics, complainers, gossipers, and disgruntled people in church life, business life, and our personal lives. The question is can you stay on track? Can you remain focused and not stop while there's noise, or do you have to tell everyone to be quiet for you to perform?

Mark Twain said, "Noise proves nothing. Often a hen who has laid an egg cackles as if she had laid an asteroid."

The devil is always making noise to distract you from your mission and commitments in life. The noise may sound like doubt or temptation. The noise may cause you to feel like a nobody or as if you can't do something. The noise may say, "Who do you think you are?" or "It will never happen."

Successful athletes know the importance of ignoring the noise. A pitcher on the mound, a quarterback in a huddle, a basketball player shooting a free throw, and a track star on the starting blocks are all very familiar with a particular ability. It's called zoning out—blocking the noise to focus on the task.

Your body is a living organism. How do you know that you're alive? You make noise. You breathe, cough, sneeze, and expel gas. When your body makes unacceptable noises like choking, vomiting, screams of pain, moans, or groans, there's a more serious problem that needs to be addressed.

It's said that within every organization, there will always be 10% to 15% noise makers (complainers). Should we silence everyone? Should we address the noise? Should we be concerned, overwhelmed, or fear the noise? Should we correct everything that's not quiet? I don't think we should, unless it's destructive, harmful, or louder than 10% to 15% of the people. Doing so may manifest a greater problem. We are to confront with wisdom, grace, and good counsel.

If someone doesn't like something in the church and is making noise about it, I don't overreact. I assess the noise level and keep doing what God told me to do. It's interesting that chatter or noise decreases or never rises above a certain level.

Don't fall for the statements, "Everybody is saying…," "Everybody is doing…," or "Everybody knows." That is noise, but it may be acceptable noise, which will always exist when you're doing a good or godly work. How it makes you feel may bait you into becoming discouraged, quitting, or overreacting.

Don't be fearful, thinking that you must control the noise level. Just evaluate it. Hear, listen, and see if there's any truth in what's being said and decide what attention you will give to it.

In 1 Corinthians 14:10, the Bible tells us that there are many different voices (noises), and they all have meaning, so the key is discerning the noise.

Jesus dealt with noise from disgruntled, critical religious leaders, yet He kept to His mission. Sometimes, the noise was ignored, and sometimes the noise was addressed.

Be discerning because addressing the noise all the time can cause more damage than good. People that you think hear the noise and those you believe are bothered by it may not even be aware of it. However, how you handle the noise may impact them.

Remember, noise isn't a bad thing. It goes along with the work you're doing. Gaining a great understanding and perspective helps you to keep performing.

Steve Jobs said, "Don't let the noise of others' opinions drown out your own inner voice."

REFLECTION QUESTIONS | Acceptable Noise Level

1. Can you work with noise?

2. What type of noise bothers you?

3. Whose noise bothers you?

4. Do you overreact to noise? Explain.

5. Do you know the difference between acceptable and unacceptable noise?

Action Item
If you don't do well with noise, work remotely from a place that's loud this week. Practice blocking out noise. If you prefer noise, work somewhere quiet.

AMBITION
Good, Bad, or Is It All the Same?

Have you ever heard phrases like, "Get going," "Shoot for the stars," "Aim High," "Go for the gold," or "Go for it"? Are these statements always good?

Often, the mindset for success or what's taught about ambition is, "It's never enough," "Go bigger," or "Get more." This way of thinking has a good side, but it also has an unattractive or bad side. People can be ambitious at the cost of being selfish, arrogant, braggadocios, big-headed, rude, or overly driven.

False ambition can have you living by comparison and competition. False ambition can make you lose sight of what or who's important. It'll have you dealing with competing priorities.

False ambition can change a kind, generous, thoughtful person into a driven person who wants to win at all costs. They'll cheat, lie, and connive to achieve. That's because false ambition takes without asking God's permission. It takes without acknowledging God in the decision.

C.J. Mahaney said, "Individuals motivated by self-interest, self-indulgence, and a false sense of self-sufficiency pursue selfish ambition for self-glorification."

The Bible reveals that the disciples of Jesus argued about who was the greatest among them. They were trying to outdo, outshine, and overshadow each other. Jesus had to correct their attitude.

There's nothing wrong with trying to achieve, be your best, and set high standards, but the end goal is to bring pleasure to Christ, help people, and be a blessing to your family. If my ambition—what I'm putting all my time, effort, and energy into—isn't drawing me close to my family but rather away from them and threatening the peace in my home, my ambition must be reconsidered.

We can disguise ambition and say, "I'm innocent," or "my motives are right," and be lying or deceiving ourselves, especially when it comes to spiritual matters or churchy ambitions. They can start innocent, but the next thing you know, they're driving you, controlling you, dominating you, and changing you.

False ambition talks to you and says, "You need me," "You have to do this," "You can't stop," "Act this way," "Be as proud as a peacock," "You are somebody," "You are special," "You are elite," and "You're doing this for your family."

I believe self-awareness and accountability are essential for detecting false ambition from good ambition. When do you evaluate yourself? How do you correct yourself? When do you examine your motives, attitude, heart, and actions? Who talks to you and tells you the gospel truth about how you are behaving or changing?

Motive is huge in discerning false ambition from good ambition. I've often asked myself the following in my church dealings: "Diego, why do you want to hire this person or hire more staff?" "Diego, why don't you come into a meeting or a room on time?" "Diego, why do you have to tell people who you know, where you've been, or what you've accomplished?" "Diego, what is your reason for doing this, wanting this, having this?" "Diego, is this too much?" "Diego, who have you been listening to?" "Diego, who has been influencing you?" "For what reason, Diego?" "Then what, Diego?"

Consider what Jesus thinks about your motives and actions. If you don't know, it's an excellent question to ask Him.

I can use many examples to speak on this subject, but I believe you get the picture. I will end with a thought that we all can identify with. How many politicians started with good intentions to help people but succumbed to corrupt ambition? How many lawyers, doctors, teachers, businessmen/women, and preachers did the same?

REFLECTION QUESTIONS | Ambition - Good, Bad, or Is It All the Same?

1. Why do you want what you want?

2. Are you an ambitious person?

3. Have you ever been guilty of false ambition?

4. How would you tell the difference between bad and good ambition?

5. What or who do you have in your life to confront good/bad ambition?

<u>Action Item</u>
Take the next steps to bring an idea to fruition. If you feel blocked, reach out to someone who can help steer you in the right direction.

IT GETS HOT SOMETIMES

You may have heard the saying, "If you can't stand the heat, get out of the kitchen." It's also been said that in difficulties, crises, and hot times, people will either take the stance of fight or flight.

Hot times are the crises, adversities, and tough times we must navigate that aren't desired or predictable. However, they must be faced with great wisdom and composure. Being a leader who makes logical decisions during a crisis is a learned practice; it is a calculated decision.

You may have heard the phrase, "Remain calm, cool, and collected in an emergency or accident." How many people do that, and how realistic is that? Well, in the case of firefighters, police officers, and military personnel, keeping your wits about you and your head on straight is imperative.

In high-pressure situations, we're often told, "Just don't panic," but that is often easier said than done. However, liken a crisis to a horror movie scene where the scary monster enters a house where people are hiding in a dark corner. When it gets near them, one of them screams and takes off running. I think you know what happens next to that individual.

During a crisis, seek a variety of advice, opinions, and ideas to come up with the most accurate information. You don't want only one opinion or one narrative from one point of view. Weigh the pros and cons. Ask yourself, "If I do one thing or another, what could possibly happen?"

The first thing I think about when met with a crisis is, *This crisis caught me off guard, but it didn't catch Jesus off guard. He has a plan and has made provision for this tragic event.*

In recent years, we've had to navigate political unrest, racial tension, immigration issues, and COVID-19. None of those were fun because we would likely offend 50% of the crowd, and 50% would love us. Amid the crises, questions came to mind like, *What should I do or what should I say? Should I post something or react to what's going on? Should I comment on the issue?* These are thoughts every leader may have had. Some likely weren't expecting to answer them or didn't know what to do because they didn't have 100% certainty.

We are all emotional, passionate, feelings-driven people, but this cannot play a part when making decisions in a crisis. How you feel, what you want to do, what you don't want to do, and what you like can't always be how you make a tough call. It requires a sensitive, healthy, well-developed conscience or conviction, which can help lead you through difficult times. You can properly decide and advise if you have a clear understanding. That happens when you calm down the noise, get to a quiet place, and listen.

Here are a few questions to consider: What does the Bible say about the issues you're facing? What has God called you to do (church or business)? What is the culture of your church? What can it handle or not handle? Have you talked about the issue before? Have you reacted to similar issues in the past? What is your track record on the matters at hand; what can you draw from the past?

I believe everyone has the right to choose the course they'll take in life. It's not my job to make people choose my path. People will choose opinions and verdicts different from mine. I have decided to be who I am before controversies or views are expressed. If that's love, kindness, and respect, then that's what I will stick with as opposed to making an enemy because someone doesn't believe the way I do during times of crisis.

Staying true to your values, character, morals, and ethics during times of crisis allows you to see things that others are too blind to see or act upon. Furthermore, leaders are known by how they handle crises, like David before Goliath, Moses before Pharaoh, and Esther before the King of Persia. Reputations are built from crises.

Abraham Lincoln said, "I am a firm believer in the people. If given the truth, they can be depended upon to meet any national crisis. The great point is to bring them the real facts."

People experience a variety of emotions during a crisis. There may be screaming, crying, silence, blaming, attacking, fear, anger, rage, worry, and anxiety. Leaders must be confident to lead with maturity. Crises can be tremendous opportunities to teach people, lead people, reach people, save people, and, in business, think of ideas to meet new needs that are discovered during a crisis.

John F. Kennedy said, "When written in Chinese, the word 'crisis' is composed of two characters – one represents 'danger,' and one represents 'opportunity.'"

Winston Churchill said, "Never let a good crisis go to waste."

REFLECTION QUESTIONS | It Gets Hot Sometimes

1. Do you think you handle a crisis well?

2. Do you think more rationally or emotionally during a crisis?

3. Are you usually the person calming people down?

4. Tell of a time when you took charge in a crisis.

5. Decide today that in the next crisis, you'll do what first?

Action Item
This week, have the conversation you've been avoiding. Share the results of the encounter with your accountability partner.

STRUCTURE

What do a table, foundation, and beam have in common? They are structures that support the weight of something else.

Realize that we can have great ideas, dreams, and visions, but if we don't have the structures to support or contain them, they can't endure the impending pressure or weight.

A stable structure is essential, especially if you live in California, like me, where earthquakes occur.

I was with a friend recently who owns an automobile repair and restoration shop. He was showing me an old 1954 truck that was being restored. He said the owner gave him a $60,000 budget to restore the vehicle. At some point in the restoration, the owner purchased a big block 454 engine that he wanted to be placed in the vehicle so it could go fast. My friend told him it would cost another $40,000 for the alteration. The owner didn't understand, so my friend explained that he had to build a larger frame for the truck to support the weight of the larger engine.

Structure can look like time, energy, or disciplines that must be developed. It can look like human resources, including staff and volunteers. It can look like teams, advisors, mentors, coaches, counselors, lawyers, and accountants. Structure can look like consequences and repercussions, a policy involving terminations, and established boundaries.

Henry Cloud said, "Boundaries are basically about providing structure, and structure is essential in building anything that thrives."

I believe a bigger, better structure can look like thinking bigger than one has in the past. That's especially true when we consider how we process people, reach people, and lead people. It's how we market/advertise, recruit, and take in information. All of these are part of the systems, procedures, and approaches contained in structures.

Structure can look like better training; that way, we can be better equipped to go bigger.

Keep in mind that techniques, systems, and protocols can become outdated, ineffective, and obsolete. If they do, they can't take you where you're trying to go. You desperately need a bigger, stronger structure.

1 Timothy 3:1-7 references someone desiring a position or office in the church. The passage describes what that person must possess to qualify for the title, and it's a great picture of what structure looks like.

Where in your life, business, or church have you outgrown something? What is not growing or declining? What are you not able to handle or keep? Are you attracting something but not able to keep it? Is anything in your life, business, or church not working properly? You may need a new or more significant structure.

Peter Drucker said, "Mission defines strategy, and strategy defines structure."

A friend told me a story of a first-string high school linebacker. He was about six feet tall and probably weighed about two hundred pounds. He was outstanding and anxiously awaiting a great scholarship to a division one college. Another linebacker on the team, who didn't have as impressive stats as the other, had already received a scholarship to a division one college.

The linebacker with less impressive stats was picked because the coaches evaluated and deemed his height and weight would increase. They said even though he was smaller, he would eventually grow taller and bigger, and they were right. He grew to six feet, four inches, and his weight increased to two hundred and fifty pounds. He grew stronger because he had a larger, better body structure as well as desire. His structure would inevitably impact his future beyond high school football.

Unfortunately, the first-string linebacker was overlooked because recruits felt he had maxed out, tapped out, and reached his peak. I don't know if that's an accurate assessment of the first-string linebacker. I simply know structure to handle growth must be considered.

Can the people around you take you where you want to go? Can they handle the growth? Can you handle the growth?

Consider an eight-inch shark in an aquarium and an eight-foot shark in the ocean. Wouldn't you say their growth is impacted by the structure or environment in which they exist?

REFLECTION QUESTIONS | Structure

1. Are all opportunities something that should be accepted?

2. Does structure have anything to do with future opportunities, systems, or procedures?

3. Where are you developing or expanding your structure for the future?

4. Can you give an example of an outdated structure in your life?

5. What structural improvements are you working on presently?

Action Item
This week, add a new structure to your life. Make a note of the changes you experience. The new structure may be going to the gym, waking early, or mentoring. Come up with something.

ALL BY MYSELF

Every leader is forced to stand alone sometimes. It's not intentional; it's just a reality. David stood alone in front of Goliath. Nehemiah stood alone in his charge to rebuild the walls of Jerusalem. Jesus stood alone in the Garden of Gethsemane and on the cross. Esther stood alone in front of the king. Moses was alone on Mount Sinai. Daniel was alone in the lion's den.

Aloneness is not the absence of people around you; it's the absence of people who understand the weight, responsibility, expectations, and challenges it takes to succeed.

John Maxwell said, "It's lonely at the top so you better know why you are there."

Elizabeth Elliot said, "Loneliness is a required course of leadership."

I've always had a supportive wife by my side. I have amazing sons, daughters, and now grandchildren. I have colleagues, board members, and friends who stand with me and around me. I have tons of prayer warriors for whom I am eternally thankful. With all of this, I still must do some things alone.

A famous actress of yesteryear, Greta Garbo, said, "I want to be alone." Who wants that?

I stand alone in many instances. For example, it's my signature that's required on massive bank loans. I must obtain insurance on myself (key man insurance) to protect the ministry in the event of an early death. I'm the one responsible for people's employment and paychecks. I stand up in front of the church to make tough announcements like the death of a member, the immorality of an employee (rarely, thank God), financial reports, and where we stand on abortion or the sanctity of marriage, or our support for Israel. I stand alone in my prayer time to prepare myself for the work of ministry as well as my study time in the Bible.

There are things I could have delegated to others but felt I had to do myself, like some funerals, some hospital visits, some disciplinary issues involving members, or making final judgment calls after hearing all the facts and listening to the advice and counsel of others. I had to make the final decision even though I knew I wouldn't be celebrated but judged, criticized, and misunderstood.

There were decisions I had to make alone – from starting our church in 1994 to more difficult ones. For instance, I had to terminate a Spanish service/church, discontinue a Saturday service, decide against the choir wearing robes on Sunday mornings, and shut down our Bible school to go in a new direction. I felt alone when I disallowed politics in the pulpit or decided not to speak out on political issues.

There have been feelings of loneliness when attacks, battles, and strikes of the enemy rose to destroy the church. I felt alone when I contemplated what could happen or how the attack might affect our attendance and financial support. Would we shrink, dissolve, or decline as a ministry? These are real thoughts that bombarded my mind and tried to drain my emotions. You likely experienced the same feelings under similar circumstances within your business or home life.

I experienced loneliness as I imagined the outcome of a situation involving a disgruntled person who was speaking ugly untruths and posting unkind statements on social media. I've had to ponder the outcome of a particular lawsuit. We have had a few in our nearly 30 years of ministry, and you'd be surprised by why people have chosen to sue. As we were preparing a thought-out succession plan, my more recent alone thought: *What will I do next?*

I am so grateful that no matter how alone I have felt in a decision, no matter how alone I've felt in my emotions or under the pressure of expectations, I have never really been alone. God has always been by my side, and so He is with you. He is the one who never leaves us nor forsakes us.

Romans 8:31 states, "What then shall we say to these things? If God is for us, who can be against us?"

Remember, if you can't handle being alone as a leader or can't get comfortable with it, you probably won't be able to lead because aloneness is a part of the price tag. We will all feel it in some form or fashion.

REFLECTION QUESTIONS | All By Myself

1. Have you ever felt alone?

2. Where have you felt alone?

3. Can you be alone and be okay?

4. Do you recognize that all leaders feel alone sometimes?

5. What can help you not to feel so alone?

Action Item
Take a day this week to do something alone. For example, go to the theater, go to a restaurant, or take a long drive.

SUSTAINABILITY

The oak tree, giant sequoia redwood tree, and olive tree can live hundreds or thousands of years. They can outlive many other great trees. Why? Sustainability is the answer. When we consider them, our thoughts are not that they are short-term but long-term, and we think of them as permanent, not temporary.

Nishiyama Onsen Keiunkan Hotel in Japan was founded in 705 AD. The Sennen No Yu Koman, also a hotel in Japan, was founded in 717 AD. The Hoshi Ryokan Hotel in Japan was founded in 718 AD, and this family-owned business has been passed down to 46 generations. What is that? It's sustainability.

Dodger Stadium was built in 1962. Why is it still around? It's sustainability.

As I approach forty years in full-time ministry, I realize that sustainability has a part to play. Heroes of mine like Oral Roberts, Billy Graham, and Tommy Barnett, all faithful ministers, had an amazing quality to finish strong.

Here are some stats:

- The average senior pastor stays four years in a church,

- The average youth minister will remain at a church three years.
- As it relates to pastors who start ministries in their twenties, only one out of ten will reach retirement age in ministry.

depending on the denomination.

It's said that of the over 300 leaders mentioned in the Bible, only thirty percent finished their race strong. That means seventy percent fell short of God's plan. Samson didn't finish well. Eli didn't finish well. Absalom didn't finish well. Solomon didn't finish well. Demas didn't finish well. Many kings/leaders mentioned in the Bible did not finish well.

I've run many marathons, and here is what I know: Not everyone who starts the race with great desire and excitement finishes the 26.2 miles.

Every minister has heard of the Three G's—girls/guys (sexual immorality), gold (mishandling/abuse of money), and glory (arrogance, haughtiness, power-hungry). Many have succumbed to them. My friend Tony Cooke adds three more: grinch (people pressure), grind (workload), and goofiness (games, gimmicks, fads, and extremes). All threaten sustainability.

There are other snipers that stop people and ministries from sustaining and finishing, like complacency and lethargy—decline in seeking, no longer hungry for God, and unwillingness to change. That means people are just going through the motions of services. There is no newness, freshness, repentance, sacrifice, giving your best, and no extra anymore. It would be like King David not fighting battles or going to war anymore but enjoying much pleasure and leisure on his balcony.

2 Timothy 4:7 states, "I have fought the good fight, I have finished the race, I have kept the faith."

A bad marriage, where there is no unity in the calling of God, can affect an organization's sustainability. Suppose neglect, division, disunity, lack of support, or marriage is not a priority. In that case, the ministry or business may not last.

I believe a few factors can keep us in the game. For one, so that we are not disqualified, be life-long learners. That means reading, listening, asking, praying, and participating in learning opportunities. Don't be an expert who thinks they know it all. Have mentors in your life. Be comfortable with people who know more than you. Engage with bigger fish that swim in a larger aquarium than you. Let them correct you.

Always examine and evaluate yourself. Self-assess your attitude, motives, heart, and time. Have times of renewal, substantial timeouts, and interests. Have times of consecration and fasting, and let God talk to you. Make time for God. Be convinced that you are called by God. Know what you're called to do, even though, as you age, assignments may differ.

Continue to be a giver. Be generous with your time and money, especially with hurting and broken people that need you. Additionally, remain a soul-winner. Share your heart, story, and faith with the lost.

Oswald J. Smith said, "The church [Christian] that doesn't evangelize will fossilize [die]."

To have sustainability, you need the stamina of an ostrich, the hide of a rhino, the determination of an eagle, the perseverance of a camel, and the tenacity of a bad germ. To have sustainability is to have stick-to-itiveness. You stay with the assignment God has given you. That looks like people, places, and plans, and it's simply being tough and gritty.

Be like the postage stamp that sticks to the letter until it arrives at its predetermined destination.

Do you want to know why a bulldog's nose is slanted backward? It's so it can continue to breathe without letting go.

REFLECTION QUESTIONS | Sustainability

1. How long can you stay with something?

2. Do you quit easily?

3. Share the longest thing you've been committed to.

4. Where do you need to do better?

5. Are you going to finish strong?

Action Item
Repeat one of the action plans this week. Choose something you can make a part of your life's routine.

THE THREE M's

Outside of our vision, which is to Seek the Lost (making it hard for people to go to hell), Teach the Found (healing the secret wounds and silent cries of hurting people), and Send the Disciples (being a living Jesus to a dying world), there have been three dominate terms and truths that have shaped my personal life and my church/business life. I'm speaking of being multicultural, multigenerational, and multi-diverse. With my heart, I always look through these lenses. In doing anything, these three M's are what I consider. They define how I do things. I measure myself and watch my life by them.

I believe these three M's speak of one's future and relevance in life. I've heard it said that life is boring without diversity. You may want to look at your life and business relationships using these lenses.

1. Multicultural

My friendships, my board, my staff, my music, my advertisements, my witness, and my guest speakers all reflect multiculturalism. I am not attracted to one race of people, one culture of people, or one skin color, but all. I'm not tolerating people but celebrating them. They are all mutually loved, valued, respected, promoted, and used with absolutely no restrictions or boundaries. I don't think one is greater or lesser than another; one is not more important or less important.

I have always felt uncomfortable around just one race of people in a church, celebration, or event. I notice who is in the room, and I notice who is not in the room. I notice who received an invitation and who wasn't invited, who was forgotten and who was remembered, who was overlooked, and who was presented.

Often, people cater to their race, style of preaching, music, and advertisements, so that's what they attract. Sometimes, people and leaders can slow performance and participation. They say one thing, but, in reality, it's not true acceptance across the board.

All my sons married multiculturally. My grandchildren are multicultural. I never talked to my children about the race of the woman they should marry. I only spoke of the values of the woman they should marry.

Here's a thought: If you're a multicultural person, do you serve food only your race enjoys or serve at least one dish that caters to another race? Think of this literally and symbolically.

It is said that the most segregated place is the church on Sunday mornings.

2. Multigenerational

I heard someone say a pastor can effectively reach and communicate well to a fifteen-year window (fifteen years above and fifteen years below their age) and not much more.

I want in my personal life and church/business life people of different ages and demographics that I can do life with. I'm not just tolerating those of a different age but celebrating them. I'm not just catering to one but all.

Too many people and organizations get old because they only do things they like, know, and are comfortable with. They aren't willing to experience or expose themselves to what a younger generation desires. They fail to realize that people don't want to be told or managed all the time. They want opportunities to lead.

You may like hymns, but does everyone like hymns? You may be stuck on a particular communication style, language, or label for one generation and not relate to another. You can become stuck and not want to adapt to a younger generation, but their opinions matter. Their insights matter, their interpretations matter, and their advice matters. Their gifts or callings matter.

Remember, Jesus was the oldest within His group; He surrounded Himself with disciples who were younger than Him.

Let everything we are involved in represent multi-generations. Yes, they will make mistakes, but that is why you're there. Be able to attract and be knowledgeable about people of all ages. Know the needs, likes, wants, and hurts of the younger generation. Forget none, including the middle-aged and elderly.

3. Multi-diverse

To be multi-diverse, an organization should include males and females in leadership roles. Both can preach and lead without limitations.

Multi-diverse is our ability to reach, teach, and serve people—rich and poor, educated and uneducated, blue collar and white collar, Republican and Democrat. Multi-diverse is the saved, churchgoers, and believers, as well as the unsaved, non-churched, and unbelievers.

We reach and help who we attract, and it's all a part of being multi-diverse.

The Bible states in 1 Corinthians 9:22, "I have become all things to all men, that I might by all means save some." The key in this passage is diversity.

How diversified are you? You've likely heard that question asked within the finance industry; however, it applies in all areas of one's life.

The following is an acrostic for diversity: **D**ifferent **I**ndividuals **V**aluing and accepting **E**ach other **R**egardless of **S**kin color and gender, **I**ntellect, **T**alent, and **Y**ears.

These three M's—multicultural, multigenerational, and multi-diverse—have served me well. The churches and people that do them well will do well.

REFLECTION QUESTIONS | The Three M's

1. Does being around people who are different make you uncomfortable or comfortable?

2. Do you notice other races that others overlook?

3. What do your friendships look like? Who gets invited to your celebrations?

4. Do you despise or put down the younger generation?

5. How can you become more diversified?

Action Item
Go out this week and try to live each "M" in some way. Try something outside of your culture. Be intentional about learning something new from those a generation or two older or young than you. Engage in a deep conversation with someone completely different from you. That may include political, ethnic, financial, or otherwise.

TRANSITIONS

It's been said, "There can be no success without a successor." I've also heard that 96% of businesses fail after the founder leaves, and most congregations are one-generation churches.

Should a church increase, decrease, or flatline when the senior leader retires? Why is finding, investing, training, equipping, and appointing a new leader difficult? Why is it especially challenging to find one who furthers the ministry and promotes it so it can thrive in the next season and for the next generation?

Here are a couple of scriptures we can use to establish a basis.

- John 14:12 KJV states, "Greater works than these shall he do."
- 2 Timothy 2:14 tells us, "Remind them of these things...."
- 2 Timothy 2:2 KJV states, "...The same commit thou to faithful men, who shall be able to teach others...."

I wonder if all leaders think or plan as if they are interim, itinerant pastors. No matter if their service is fifty years, would they be better prepared if they thought this way when they started ministry or when they were young?

All too often, we wait too late before we think about a succession plan. We wait until we're rushed, there's a crisis or emergency. We are waiting and causing things to become disorganized, confusing, unstructured, and chaotic. Typically, outside help and advice/counsel are not sought, and responsibility falls on one person. The weight of that decision on one person is often met with no accountability. In many instances, the idea of when, how, and why is never considered or discussed.

Sometimes, emotions can cloud our thoughts, and, out of desperation, we want to believe that we have found a successor. However, honest testing, honest assessments, honest conversations, honest evaluations, and feedback are avoided, especially when it comes to one's own family. We can be blindsided into believing something or wanting something out of nepotism.

As it relates to this challenging circumstance, what can we learn? Well, for one, it usually takes longer than one thinks, and there are several factors to consider.

There is a proper time to begin the succession process. Consider the age of the senior leader. There is a window of not too young and not too old. Speaking chronologically, the age of the successor is also not too young and not too old. The successor is not a novice, but they're also not unwilling to grow because they are beyond peak years.

Methodical, thorough training is imperative for the effectiveness of the successor. It's crucial that they display effectiveness as a communicator, effectiveness in administration (finances, business, HR, budgeting, interaction with lawyers and accountants), effectiveness in people skills (sociability, friendliness, hospitality, kindness), and effectiveness in marriage and family matters. For example, whether or not the spouse can handle the responsibility may have to come into consideration. Has counseling taken place, and is the individual's family prepared?

Effectiveness in character (moral issues, ethical issues, integrity issues) and effectiveness in spiritual life (love for Jesus, strength of faith, trust, submission toward Christ with an excellent prayer life, and love for scriptures) are as important.

An appropriate vetting period should be established to observe, prove, and transition the organization from one leader to another. That will help members of the organization acclimate to the senior pastor leaving and the successor pastor stepping in. The goal is to ensure that the congregation adapts as seamlessly as possible.

A practical option would be 90% senior pastor leading and 10% successor leading. Develop a plan that includes a designated term to flip the percentages of 10% senior pastor and 90% successor leading. Again, this is an option an organization can apply to turn over responsibility a little at a time.

One of the most significant challenges I've seen is the senior leader and spouse being unprepared for the next season. That may be financial, a second career, or other interests. Because of that, he either stays too long, gets in the way, dominates, or frustrates the successor.

When the time comes to execute the official succession plan, the senior pastor must learn and begin to decrease so that the successor can increase in confidence, authority, and leadership. The senior leader must begin to see his successor as his pastor. Even though discovery and investing could have been done many years before, in the culture of how we think of church, much prayer, conversation, bonding, and fellowship must continue between the two.

The successor must honor and respect his senior pastor for all that has been stewarded into his hands. That may include personal and public gratitude and affirmation. He should continue to seek a relationship with the senior leader, who should always feel welcome to give advice or prayers because so much he worked for over his lifetime has been given to another. It may be done at the successor's discretion, but it is always gratifying when a successor remains in contact, in some form, with the previous leader.

When it's time for the process to begin, imagine it this way: The senior leader is in the driver's seat of a bus (the ministry). Over time, the bus may be filled with several potential successors. You move people from the back to the front passenger seat based on character, competency, chemistry, calling, and commitment. When you have someone in that passenger seat and you're driving the bus, move them to the driver's seat over time, and proceed with both of you having your hands on the steering wheel—lead together. It takes a secure, humble senior leader to do this, but he must understand the process and recognize that his leadership term is limited.

Both leaders must want the church/organization to thrive in the future. Tough conversations and differences in opinion will occur during this process, but don't stifle the successor. Let him or her speak openly on any subject, including matters where opinions differ. Let the successor make decisions; let them call the shots, even if their style differs from yours.

I've committed to the succession process, and it has served me well.

REFLECTION QUESTIONS | Transitions

1. Do you have a successor?

2. How did you or how are you recruiting and developing successors?

3. Have you put together a clear and precise plan?

4. When will you pass the baton?

5. Have you prepared yourself financially and emotionally for the transition?

Action Item
Start a new tradition in your household or among your family members. Select a family heirloom that will be passed down to future generations.

WITHOUT FAITH

Chuck Ford said, "Faith is to be persuaded of God's will in a matter and that you act accordingly."

Martin Luther King Jr. said, "Faith is taking the first step even when you don't see the whole staircase."

My whole church life and church world, as a personal believer in Christ, as well as my job/career, has all been done by faith in my God. I have learned, and I'm still learning, how to trust, depend on, acknowledge, require, and put my confidence in God. He is the one I give credit to and boast about. He's the God who gave me the faith to do what I did and am doing.

I started our church in the living room of our little house with twelve people. I had no promises, no commitments, no backing, no marketing, and no team. It was just my wife and me. That was way before the internet, fundraising platforms, and social media to post advertisements and recruit. Our church has become an organization that exists to help start churches and finance churches, for which I'm grateful.

I had little knowledge about how to start or build a church. We didn't have financial support or any money in the bank to help us. I had no mentors, pastors, coaches, or teachers to advise me on what to do or not do. I had very few friends or colleagues because of how I was asked to leave my former church. All my friends and community were at that church.

I suffered a loss of income. I experienced financial challenges and family crises that were horribly overwhelming to bear. I had no health insurance for myself or my family. I was employed at a warehouse that didn't provide insurance. Additionally, I didn't have enough money to go on a nice family vacation, buy a nice car or a couple of suits.

I had a lot of hurt, unforgiveness, and bitterness in my heart. I had a lot of insecurity and low self-esteem issues that prevailed in my life. I didn't feel I had the best appearance, charisma, intelligence, or people skills; I still don't.

I had no business skills, accounting skills, or real estate knowledge. I had no experience as an employer, proprietor, or manager. I hadn't read a lot of books. I didn't like to read because of my failures in school and the challenges I experienced in remembering what I read.

Over the years in ministry, I've had fears. I've experienced betrayal from members and staff. I've been criticized and judged. I've been lonely and discouraged. I've felt overwhelmed and pressured.

There have been times when I didn't know what I was doing, nor did I ask what to do or how to get something done. There have been times of crisis, emergency, and maybe even panic. I've felt disqualified in managing situations that were undoubtedly out of my league and above my pay grade.

2 Corinthians 4:8 states, "We are hard-pressed on every side, yet not

crushed; we are perplexed, but not in despair."

I was appointed president of a school, and I have no degree and attended only one and one-half years of junior college, but God....

I've had health challenges. I cracked the C5 vertebrae in my neck and was paralyzed for five minutes. I had to wear a halo device, but God.... I had terminal stage 4 kidney cancer, but God.... I experienced an emotional breakdown (PTS) and cried out of control, but God....

What has been the defining factor in my life? It's nothing I was born with or bought. It was not a seminar, conference, meeting, or lesson taught. It wasn't acquired in a classroom, textbook, retreat, or self-help center. It was faith, pure faith, and nothing but faith. And, it's not the kind of faith that's just a belief in God, but an active faith that's exercised. It's an action that turns to God, knowing He's the only one who can bring me to a place, through a place, and out of a place.

The Bible says faith is the thing that pleases God, and He rewards it. For a Christian to be successful, he needs it. We are to walk in a state of faith, not by what we see, feel, or sense.

As I look at the success we've experienced as a ministry and the things we've acquired that the world can measure, like the size of a building, the size of a budget, the size of a congregation, assets, platforms, and followers, I can say that all this is because of faith.

It was faith like Peter's who, against all odds, when it didn't make sense, when logic may have been racing through his thoughts, got out of the boat and walked on water to Jesus with few guarantees, agreements, assurances, or pledges. What Peter had was Jesus calling him forward and backing him, and that's enough for me too.

Andrew Bonar said, "God's part is to put forth power; our part is to put forth faith."

As I sum this up, finding a promise, holding to a promise, and standing on a promise from God's word, the Bible, is truly what gives you faith to do the impossible.

REFLECTION QUESTIONS | Without Faith

1. What have you ever done by faith, trusting God for the outcome?

2. Do you require guarantees before you trust God?

3. What does faith in God look like to you?

4. How do you get or strengthen your faith?

5. Where can you start to exercise more faith?

Action Item
Take the next step to bring your idea to fruition. You should be close to launching your idea at this point.

EXAMINE YOURSELF

Arrogance, ignorance, and presumptions are the actions and attitudes of the little.

2 Corinthians 13:5 states, "Examine yourselves as to whether you are in the faith. Test yourselves. Do you not know yourselves, that Jesus Christ is in you?—unless indeed you are disqualified [to lead]."

There's the DISC test, Strength Finder test, Enneagram test, and many more personality assessments, but here's a thought: Know the people around you better because they will make you better. Don't treat people like you treat yourself. Treat them better. Don't look at people the way you view or think about yourself. Do better.

My mistake was thinking I didn't need applause, praise, or encouragement to do what I do, and because I didn't need it or do it for myself, I didn't need to do that for others.

Just because you don't need something doesn't mean the people around you are like you or aren't in need. People aren't wired like you. They don't have your strengths, gifts, talents, needs, wants, or desires. Don't treat them like you treat yourself. Know the people that you work with. It's said that a fool presumes where a wise man investigates.

Criss Jami said, "A pure heart does not demean the spirit of an individual; it, instead, compels the individual to examine his spirit."

Study the people in your life. Ask the people around you what they like and don't like to receive from you or about you. Understand the people around you. I know this can feel awkward and unnecessary, especially as an employer, because you think it's an employee's job to know you but it's not your job to know them. That is wrong and not servant-leadership. Jesus knew his disciples and treated them accordingly. Consider how He motivated, encouraged, inspired, and corrected them.

That was a definite do-over for me. I'm just a hard-wired, self-motivated, get-the-job-done, driven person who doesn't need much to do the job. Not everyone has my personality, my upbringing, my countenance, my history, my resolve, my story, my good fortune, my parents, my helpers, and my friends.

Give people not just the resources, paychecks, bonuses, benefits, titles, and offices they need. Give them your words, gifts, ears, heart, time, encouragement, and love. Think of it in terms of "it goes with the job." You offer relationship and friendship in your life, right? If not, then maybe you need to relook at your leadership style.

You're not to be a dictator, ignorant, controlling, or demanding leader. We all know leaders like that. We recognize our individual strengths, personalities, and giftings, but we are to accept and celebrate unique qualities in others as well. If our make-up or style becomes why we don't think of others' feelings or value, view as important, know them, and hear them, it can lead to a one-sided relationship. It can also lead to a high turnover rate. You then become a person who is tolerated, not celebrated, and maybe feared but not liked. You are talked about behind your back rather than face to face like a friend.

Keep in mind that it's one thing to build an organization, but it's another animal to hold it together and keep it going.

We often work on the front end of relationships to ensure they are the right fit for our team, organization, or staff. Unfortunately, that usually is where the work or diligence ends. We are nice, friendly, and outgoing in the beginning to win them over. How about working on and maintaining the back end to ensure we are leading our people with great understanding and being the best version of ourselves.

Choose to be completely observant and not naïve about your leadership style. You may be a demanding, driven, high-capacity leader, but you should also be a sensitive, compassionate, and generous leader. Again, don't treat people like you treat yourself.

Here's a strong question: Would you like to be your employee, friend, or mate?

REFLECTION QUESTIONS | Examine Yourself

1. Do you put in all the work on the front end of a relationship to attract people and then neglect them deeper into the relationship?

2. Do you treat people like you treat yourself? Do you treat others worse or better?

3. Have you ever been frustrated because you expected people to be you, but they are not?

4. Where can you start to change?

5. What type of leader do you believe you are?

Action Item
Review your action items and note the growth you've experienced since you began reading this book. Share this information with your accountability partner.

SCALING

Jesus had twelve disciples, and then He had 70, 120, and 500 followers. Then it grew bigger—hundreds of millions or billions; that's scaling.

Ginni Rometty said, "We're about to scale something now that couldn't have been scaled before."

Have you ever seen scaffolding on the side of a building, like a high rise? It's made up of planks and metal bars stacked along the side of a building under construction or repair. It allows workers to scale the outside of the structure safely and move upward or downward from one floor to the next.

When is it time to scale your church or business safely? What does it take to scale your operation? Are you ready to scale just because you're successful in one area, field, or endeavor?

Scaling is the strategy of preparing and planning to go bigger or increase in an area. Scaling can be hiring employees, buying property, building structures, franchising or acquiring a new business, expanding a portfolio, or moving locations or operations toward a new opportunity or arena.

I remember asking a friend who owns three car dealerships when he was going to buy a fourth. He said the car company is begging him to take on another dealership because of his quality of excellence. He said he couldn't until he built a better, stronger, broader infrastructure. He told me no matter how much he wanted to, or others wanted him to, he wouldn't be able to sustain the same quality as the three in operation without being stronger. Wow! That's wisdom in scaling.

Tavis Smiley said, "Why don't we scale up those things that do work."

Over the years, we have faced the challenges of scaling too soon or too late. Just because someone else was or wasn't scaling, should we?

We have grown to multiple campuses, hired hundreds of staff over the years, purchased real estate to expand, and taken on more vision, including multiple services (seven a week at one time: one Saturday, four Sunday morning, one Sunday night, and one Wednesday), and that does not include Friday night prayer or special events for men, women, youth, and children.

Scaling should be considered if needs are unmet, customer service is suffering, volunteers are being overworked and undersupplied, or there's inconsistency in volunteering (can't carry the weight). Scaling should happen when you're running out of seats or space to accommodate people or out of room to house a product.

When quality and excellence begin to suffer, the leadership and staff are being overtaxed and overtasked, or priorities are being neglected, scaling may be necessary.

Scaling may be required when the leader is not functioning at their best to dream, problem-solve, or do whatever they are required to do that can't be delegated. That may apply in the business world, church world, or one's spiritual life.

Scaling should happen when we have the right personnel to handle the growth, and proper training has been done so that they have complete confidence.

Scaling should also happen when you have the financial stability or reserves to handle a larger budget. Scaling requires the proper technology to communicate and facilitate well. The organization should have the appropriate resources/materials to meet the demands to expand. Maintaining high-quality service as you grow, not losing customers, and upholding your values are essential. If not, you may overextend yourself and adversely impact quality.

Shawn Fanning said, "I think the most difficult thing had been scaling the infrastructure. Trying to support the response we had received from our users and the number of people that were interested in using the software."

Again, you can have amazing growth or fruit but not be ready to scale. Having the agreement of a board of advisors, spousal support, family support, and the support of friends is essential. Enlist their opinions on scaling.

REFLECTION QUESTIONS | Scaling

1. Have you ever thought about scaling?

2. When is a good time to scale?

3. Can scaling increase your growth?

4. What hinders you from scaling?

5. What needs to be scaled?

Action Item
What is one thing you can do with your eyes closed (figuratively speaking)? How can you take that skill to the next level? Take this week to do what you can to grow your skill. That may include evolving it into something better or teaching someone how to do what you do.

RESILIENT AND RESOURCEFUL

Proverbs 6:6 TPT states, "When you're feeling lazy, come and learn a lesson from this tale of the tiny ant. Yes, all you lazybones, come learn from the example of the ant and enter into wisdom."

The ant has many characteristics to be admired, including selflessness, tirelessness, cleverness, strength, and teamwork. There are two characteristics observed in ants that I consider excellent life skills to possess—resilience and resourcefulness.

Resilience is the ability to keep on keeping on, not allowing life's difficulties, troubles, or unexpected disappointments to stop you.

Resilient people, when they have multiple doors shut in their faces, believe the next door will be the one that remains open for them. Everyone gets knocked down, but resilient people won't and don't stay down. Like a ball held underwater, they pop up again. They have an amazingly confident spirit.

I've heard it said that there are three types of people—the pessimist, the realist, and the optimist. The pessimist assumes it won't happen, so why try or even start. Realists think it might happen, but they first consult the odds, facts, conditions, circumstances, and situations. The optimist believes it will happen, despite disadvantages, inabilities, inadequacies, opposition, and obstacles.

Over the years that I've been in ministry, I've come to realize that I don't accept someone saying "No, I can't or won't" very well. As a matter of fact, I don't accept no's very well. If you tell me something can't be done, I see that as a challenge, not a finality. It's a challenge to learn, grow, change, and train hard.

I'm not the most gifted person. I often think of myself as the "one talent" guy in the Bible instead of the "five talents" guy due to my inabilities. I could allow my lack of skills, knowledge, or resources to stop me from obeying or moving forward with my vision or the dreams God placed in my heart.

Most things don't come fast or easy, but they are achievable. That includes being approved for a challenging loan, buying property, erecting a building, writing books, producing a television show, or leading a multicultural, multigenerational, and multi-diverse church.

Your aspirations may not be your reality today, but they can be one day. Resilience says, "If not today, then tomorrow. If not now, someday."

Martin Luther King Jr. said, "If you can't fly, then run; if you can't run, then walk; if you can't walk, then crawl, but whatever you do, you have to keep moving forward."

Resourcefulness, the second notable characteristic of the ant, is finding a way and using everything to one's advantage. It's easily adjusting and adapting to changes. It's thinking on your feet, being inventive, imaginative, creative, and solutions-driven.

Resourceful people say, "This is the hand that's been dealt to me, and I'm going to make the most of it." They won't let excuses for not being able to do something stop them. They don't rationalize or justify why they can't do something. They don't blame others for their failures but take full responsibility for their actions.

Resourceful people find tools, ingredients, and people, such as contractors, leaders, etc. (you get the picture), to get the job done. Resourceful people are like the TV show *MacGyver* or *Man vs. Wild* with Bear Grylls. They have a knack for solving complex problems in a spontaneous and unconventional way. They find a way out of the most challenging circumstances using critical thinking and, sometimes, not taking no for an answer.

I remember one time, while looking for property to build the church, we encountered challenges locating property through a realtor. I asked my assistant to go on a search to see if she could find a property. I also decided to drive around the city and asked others to do the same.

The Bible speaks of asking, seeking, and knocking, which are good actions, and it's all in the attitude.

Guess what? We located a property, not through a professional realtor but through stubborn resilience and resourcefulness.

There's an old saying, "The show must go on," but that can only happen for the resilient and resourceful.

REFLECTION QUESTIONS | Resilient and Resourceful

1. How resilient and resourceful are you?

2. Share a time when being resilient/resourceful yielded positive results.

3. How can you strengthen your level of resilience/resourcefulness?

4. Can you achieve success without being resilient or resourceful?

5. Who can help you be more resilient and resourceful?

Action Item
Take one or two resilient and resourceful people to lunch. Ask them at least five questions to learn how they developed those qualities.

ENGAGING IN THE HARD CONVERSATIONS

One of my favorite movie scenes is from *A Few Good Men*. Lt. Kaffee (Tom Cruise) asks Col. Jessep (Jack Nicholson), "Did you order the Code Red?" The courage of Kaffee to ask the Colonel when his career could be jeopardized for questioning a decorated officer adds to the drama in the scene. It's a great display of leadership.

Jeanne Phillips said, "Sometimes the most important conversations are the most difficult to engage in."

Linda Lambert said, "One good conversation can shift the direction of change forever."

Anyone can have fun, easy conversations with people where there's laughter, jokes, shared interests, and where nothing feels threatening, intimidating, or uncomfortable. In life, however, sometimes you must be able to have hard conversations with people that deal with expectations, responsibilities, and disappointment. Sometimes, you must talk about consequences for one's actions or failure, consequences for one's behavior or damages.

Hard conversations can involve employee terminations due to cutbacks, layoffs, downsizing, and elimination of a position. It could be the termination of a toxic relationship in your life. None of these are fun but carry a lot of internal anguish, especially when directed at close friends, family members, spouses, and children. Yuck! Right? But you can't be a leader and not be willing to have tough conversations with people. Avoidance, passivity, ignorance, tolerance, and shyness are not attractive traits.

Is there a difference between being a winner or wimpy, being courageous or a coward, or being straightforward or retreating from hard conversations?

I wonder if it was easy for Jesus to confront James' and John's anger issue when they wanted to hurt the Samaritan who rejected Jesus. Was it easy for Jesus to tell Peter he would deny Him before the rooster crowed? Was it easy for Him to talk directly to the hypocrisy of the religious leaders of His day? What about confronting the rich young ruler who idolized money, knowing he wouldn't change but would walk away sad? What about the disciples mentioned in John 6:66 who were following Him but left and were never fans of His ministry again because He spoke hard words?

I've had to deal with unwanted, unwelcomed conversations with a family member who was employed at our church regarding a difference in theological beliefs and how they were influencing others in the church and causing confusion. I had to approach another family member who was very rude and disrespectful to his fellow employees. Both cases involving family members didn't go well. They both quit and left the church.

I've had to confront immorality with an employee who was lying and stealing. I had to have hard conversations with influential members of the church who were outstanding financial givers but exhibited a lack of Christian character. None of these were exciting, and if they were, there is a greater issue that I'd have to deal with; a flaw that would require confrontation and change.

The Bible uses words like "rebuke." When are we supposed to do that? It tells us to "convince." How do we do that? It contains the word "reproof." Why do we do that? It tells us to "admonish." Where do we do that? "Correct" is stated. What is that?

If you have a relationship with someone, if you are an authority figure over someone, if you love someone, or if you are in charge of someone and notice an error, falsehood, or destructive habits, behaviors, or lifestyle, don't you have a responsibility to have a hard conversation?

We cannot have an excellent moral character until we are able to have hard conversations with people with humility, love, respect, confidence, and boldness. We have a responsibility to protect and help them as well as our churches and businesses. If we cannot do our part, we will never become responsible leaders. Instead, we will reproduce and condone poor behavior, affecting productivity, growth, and much more.

REFLECTION QUESTIONS | Engaging In the Hard Conversations

1. Do you remember having a hard conversation with someone?

2. How did the conversation turn out?

3. What did you learn from it?

4. What happens to us and others when we don't engage in hard conversations?

5. What does inaction say about an individual who avoids hard conversations?

Action Item
Take the last steps needed to finalize your idea and launch it. That may involve having the conversations only you can have, whether with yourself or someone else.

EPILOGUE

Kalu Ndukwe Kalu said, "The things you do for yourself are gone when you are gone, but the things you do for others remain as your legacy."

Pericles said, "What you leave behind is not what is engraved in stone monuments, but what is woven into the lives of others."

Billy Graham said, "The greatest legacy one can pass on to one's children and grandchildren is not money…but rather a legacy of character and faith."

As I finish this book on what I think has built our church/ministry, I also want to consider the things that I have valued, things that I would love to teach to my grandchildren and pass on to another generation of leaders.

I love words like disciplines, values, morals, ethics, integrity, character, faithfulness, habits, dedication, standards, exampleship, commitment, truth, indebtedness, gratitude, generosity, perseverance, loyalty, and love. Additionally, I've listed some favorite sayings or adages. Some may be topics I wrote about, and some may not have been covered, but here they are.

1. See the need and take the lead. Don't wait; you take charge and do it if it's in your heart to do.

2. Make every day a big day. Give your best; finish what you

promise.

3. It takes years to earn a good reputation, and it can take minutes to lose it. Be watchful; don't be stupid.

4. Live intentionally, not accidentally. Prepare, plan, have a strategy, and limit the crises and emergencies that you can.

5. Pray it forward. When tempted to make a major decision, think about the effects and consequences.

6. Be tougher than your toughest day. When the devil attacks you, do whatever it takes to obey God.

7. Don't make major decision in the valley but on the mountaintop. When you're down, don't decide anything. Wait until you're at a good place.

8. Stop internalizing what happened, why it happened, and where it happened. Learn from situations. Forgive, move on, and let go.

9. Always pray for people that hurt you. Keep your heart right. Don't keep score.

10. Never burn bridges of relationships because you may need them in the future. Keep the door open for reconciliation.

11. Always have a second income. Have streams of income (personal and ministry) besides tithes and offerings or a paycheck.

12. Engage in futuring. Always have an eye, ear, and conversation about what the future will look like.

13. What you do sets a precedence. If you do something for one,

do it for all. No favoritism.

14. Always be spotting leaders. Consider others for projects, ideas, consultation, advice, and relationships.

15. Pay employees not just to do but to reproduce, and try to pay them well.

16. Don't just have meetings. Have effective meetings with agendas, expectations, calendars/schedules, updates, prayer, collaboration, recaps, and celebrate wins.

17. Hire slowly, fire quickly. It will limit heartache. We seem to hire for IQ and fire for EQ.

18. Maintain a strict financial budget. Save 10-20% and pay more than the interest payment by paying down the principle.

19. Develop a fierce appetite to grow and learn. Change and get better.

20. The church doesn't do anything less than the world's standards but better. Nothing should be average or just okay.

21. Fight for God's kingdom. Don't be pushed around by an organization that wants to abuse, misuse, or neglect the church.

22. Enjoy the journey. Know that it will go fast. Smile more, laugh more, have great conversations, sing more, try fun stuff, vacation well, hold hands with your spouse and kids, take walks, and sit and relax. Lastly, love Jesus massively because He is so proud of you.

23. Don't let your passion drown out your compassion. That's when people don't think you care.

24. Walk slowly through the crowd. Be available and accessible. Listen, talk, and understand.

25. Never forget those that helped you arrive where you are. Stay close and compassionate toward them. Always have time for them.

26. Be extremely resilient. Rebound, reengage, renew, recharge, re-enlist, recommit, revive.

www.ingramcontent.com/pod-product-compliance
Lightning Source LLC
Chambersburg PA
CBHW050856160426
43194CB00011B/2181